Bob Garratt is Cha[...] [...]tional in
London and of Organization Development [...] in Hong
Kong. He has a global consultancy advising on corporate
governance, director development and strategic thinking. He
[...] founder [...] other [...] Hong Kong [...] to create the
[...] C[...] Co[...] [...]ng the Ca[...] [...]ssion H[...]
[...] [...]. [...] Su[...] Te[...]g [...]gy Medicine,
[...]
Developing Strategic Thought which h[...] [...] [...]
Fish Rots From [...] Head.

The Twelve Organizational Capabilities

Valuing People at Work

BOB GARRATT

HarperCollinsBusiness

HarperCollins*Publishers*
77–85 Fulham Palace Road,
Hammersmith, London W6 8JB

www.**fire**and**water**.com/business

This paperback edition 2000
1 3 5 7 9 8 6 4 2

First published in Great Britain by
HarperCollins*Publishers* 1999

ISBN 0 00 638896 5

Set in Linotype Sabon

Printed and bound in Great Britain by
Clays Ltd, St Ives plc

To Sally

without whose insatiable desire to find out
what is really going on in organizations
this book would not have been possible.

Contents

Introduction

Why are most organizations incapable of delivering their purpose effectively, efficiently, and with the active co-operation of those who work in them? Private and publicly listed companies, public-sector and parastatal bodies, charities and not-for-profits are frequently criticized, both for not looking ahead effectively and for being inefficient and customer-unfriendly in the delivery of their services or goods.

By failing to balance effectiveness with efficiency many organizations lose their ability to control and develop their Organizational Capabilities – the ability to make things happen in the way intended by directors and senior managers, and with the active co-operation of employees. Effective and efficient enterprises must possess the strategic capability of giving clear direction combined with competent strategic thinking, and the ability to implement strategies through systematic and co-operative feedback, leading to continuous learning at operational level. Most organizations that I have encountered are nothing like that.

Many chairmen, chief executives, directors and senior managers will pronounce blithely on the time and money spent developing their organization's purpose, vision and values, yet they rarely bother to check carefully what has been communicated, understood and committed to by their staff. Consequently, the direction-givers do not know, nor can they measure, whether they have the systems or the corporate energy to deliver their intentions, in short, whether there is sufficient Organizational Capability available. Directors and senior managers often have a nagging fear that when they pull the levers of power they will find that they are not connected.

Short-circuits at this crucial interface between strategy and implementation will block the organization's ability to learn and develop. If this process is repeated, then it will become a habit, and such habits lead eventually to incapable organizations and corporate collapse. Incapable organizations are unable to adapt to changes in their external and internal environments. Before collapsing they under-perform, become incapable of effective delivery of their goods or services, customers and clients move away, the staff fail to focus their energy, avoid risks and blame others, the emotional climate becomes soured, and learning ceases. Each of these issues is measurable, and together they form the basis for the twelve elements of Organizational Capability.

Why are such collapses so common in so many countries? Why do employees around the world feel that the organizations they work for have so many of these non-learning characteristics? The lack of any robust intellectual framework for, and language of, the fundamental human process of 'organizing' leads to this global problem. While executives increasingly understand the logic of business, they still fail to grasp that there is a complementary field of 'organizing'. Economic logic and the rationality of systems must be balanced with social and emotional processes before an effective organization can be formed. Each side interacts with the other to create positive, or negative, feedback.

This book attempts to illustrate and rectify such problems. It is intended as a strong antidote to the current fashion for thoughtlessly downsizing and rightsizing, which eventually leads firms to capsize. There are now so many examples of the disastrous consequences of the unthinking application of such over-rational, action-fixated and cost-cutting approaches to organizational change, that the damage created by them can now begin to be assessed.

Prior to such analysis two fundamental aspects of organizing – the linking of elements to create a living system – need to be emphasized. First, is the assumption that there is a 'hard' side to any organization. In the executive thinking process this operates at the level of logic, rationality and structure. The 'hard' side provides direction-givers and managers with reasonable levels of certainty about the likely consequences of their deployment of scarce resources, which allows them to plan to achieve their purpose and targets. It also gives them sources of formal power over those they employ. This 'hard' side allows the *efficiency* of the organization to be measured, usually through financial results, and is often considered the only way in which its performance can be assessed.

Second, and of equal importance to the 'hard' side, there is a 'soft' side to organizations, which comprises human energies, emotions and learning which is continuous and motivating. These elements are rarely measured. They are quantifiable, but because most directors and managers think of them as invisible and are not aware of their impact, they are rarely assessed on a regular and rigorous basis, and are frequently discounted as 'proper' measures of business results. Yet they affect dramatically organizational *effectiveness* – the external perception of the organization by its customers, suppliers and other stakeholders. Even when these factors are assessed they are usually given much lower priority than financial measures of performance. The twelve elements of Organizational Capability set out to correct this imbalance of measures.

These 'soft' aspects are the missing key determinants of short-, medium- and long-term Organizational Capability and performance. The Organizational Capability needed to attain such performance is achieved by the continuous critical review and rebalancing of the 'hard' and 'soft' sides by the directors and senior managers, but as there is as yet no agreed language to describe the 'soft' sides of organizations, and as so little is taught about them, most directors and managers are forced to over-rely on the 'hard', financial side. This leaves a massive gap in their ability to describe and use organizational competences. The situation is gradually changing, as appreciation of the benefits and problems of working with the complementary, 'soft', human, side of organizing begins to grow. In a world of increasing uncertainty, complexity and seeming chaos, even the hard sciences seem to be embracing the idea of 'softness'. When physicists and mathematicians are at ease talking of 'chance as cause', then the old Newtonian certainties are obviously under serious review.

Such considerations are also appearing in the apparently 'hard' world of finance. The international speculator and philanthropist George Soros was reported in The *Financial Times*[1] musing on the problems of the Millennium Bug in computers, which he feared could lead to a meltdown in financial systems:

> The *behaviour* of market players is as much about markets as the so-called fundamentals. And it is the human factors as much as the mechanical factor which will trouble computer-vulnerable governments, agencies, power companies, water companies, airlines and banks over the coming year.

It is the 'soft', human, aspects which can both cause the problems, and get us out of them. The 'hard' systems are only capable of obeying orders.

Sadly, most directors and managers have been schooled in the primacy of logic, particularly economic logic, and the paramount position of hard facts and rational decision-making. This, in combination with the near-invisibility of the soft factors, and the absence of an appropriate descriptive framework, makes it difficult for them to allow that human emotions, positive or negative, can add, or detract, value from decision-taking. Instead they tend to over-focus on 'hard', short-term financial measures. The human consequences of this bottom-line, and annual budget, fixation fall into two main categories.

First, the executives not having the medium-and long-term perspective to understand the importance of such external issues as the loss of perceived quality in goods or services by consumers. Unthinking cost-cutting loses both the customer's perceived benefits of your offering, and the experience base of the organization. The consequence is a growing loss of customers. A knee-jerk reaction from many managers is to cost-cut even deeper, so further depleting the experience base. This occurs because experienced people are seen by most managers as too costly to employ compared with younger, cheaper staff. Ironically, experienced staff can be shown to be more cost-effective than less experienced ones as they tend to make fewer mistakes, stay longer, are more open to learning rather than just being 'trained', and are better at using their informal networks to get things done. But this does not show up easily if one uses only a short-term, bottom-line approach to budgeting and efficiency. Such an approach does not measure the organization's *effectiveness* as perceived by customers. This decides whether they will buy your goods or services rather than others'. Added to this, the tyranny of the unthinking application of an annual budget process can destroy the connectedness of an organization, and so disrupt the informal human networks which energize and regulate it in real time.

Measuring the gaps in Organizational Capabilities, between the reality on each dimension, and what needs to be in place for our purpose to be achieved, creates a constructive way of avoiding the present, and future, consequences of unimaginative, expedient cost-cutting. A few organizations are attempting this. Those which are find that they have to rethink rapidly their organizational, as distinct from business, processes and then gauge more rigorously and sensitively the consequences of their continuing experiences so that they can learn more about the appropriate balance between the 'hard' and the 'soft' factors. Such a rethink changes their beliefs about the positioning of their people's learning at work. Learning becomes a central Organizational Capability, and can no longer be considered simply as part of the training budget on the profit-and-loss account spend for the year – just a cost to be minimized. It becomes part of the business strategy, through its inclusion in the organization's asset base, and is reflected on the balance sheet. My present concern for many acknowledged 'quality', creative organizations – like the BBC, which in my opinion now takes an over-rational approach to organizational change – is that they can quickly and unwittingly create incapable organizations. In these, human energies are channelled away from creative endeavour, and into fighting imposed and often inappropriate organizational structures and processes. In the short term the imposed structures usually win, but in the medium to long term either the system fights back in an internal civil war, or the organization crashes.

Second, internally, there is a noticeable rise in unproductive work in increasingly incapable organizations. Typically, much more time is spent in covering up mistakes, blaming others, avoiding risks, and keeping one's head below the parapet in the often vain hope of not being blamed or not being made redundant. In the medium term this causes a significant loss of productivity and profitability across the organization. These are currently under-researched, negative aspects of the 'soft' side of organizations.

If both the external and internal negative human consequences coincide, there is a high chance that the organization will capsize, especially if the organization is following uncritically the current 'industry formula' which usually does not rate highly customers, staff, suppliers, stakeholders and, eventually, the shareholders. Then that high chance becomes a near certainty. The only question is 'When?'

Most of these problems are avoidable if directors and managers understand not only the business aspects of their enterprise but also the human, social-emotional processes of their organization – and the necessary balances to be struck between them. They can then be more sensitive to, and certain of, the *organizational* consequences of their actions. Consciously or unconsciously, directors and managers create and sustain their organization's capabilities, whether positive or negative. They create the emotional climate that gives life, meaning, energy and opportunities to their people, beyond the monthly salary.

Sadly, emotion tends to have a negative, irrational, meaning in the English language, and is avoided by most managers, who are proud to see themselves as non-emotional and data-rational. This is nonsense: emotions can be both positive and negative; the problems come from habitually using only one side of the emotions. Whatever the paper-based logic of any course of action, it must also generate positive emotional commitment from those people at whom it is aimed. As a young officer cadet, one of the most traumatic episodes for me was 'leading' my troops over the top, only to find no one emulating my reckless example. Leadership includes followership as a key element. Too many of today's leaders seem happy to lead without checking that they have followers. Measures of Organizational Capability can reveal the gaps between their aspiration and the reality in horrifying clarity.

This book challenges the current, too easily accepted, notion that financial measures, and hard logic, must always be paramount in any organization. Turning conventional business wisdom on its head, I argue that good financial results are the *consequence* of getting, and keeping, the other measures right. Organizational effectiveness, as perceived by the customers, comes before organizational efficiency, not after, and both can be measured against the twelve dimensions of Organizational Capability. I suggest a common language for organizing people's capabilities so that both business targets and the thin film of lubrication which keeps the organization working – the key social-emotional processes – may be reviewed critically and debated more openly and effectively by all those involved. This is to the customers', the staff's, the leaders', the suppliers', the stakeholders', the shareholders' and, ultimately, the organization's mutual benefit.

In writing this book I have used an apparent paradox, in that, while looking ahead towards the creation of more effective twenty-first-century organizations, it is wise also to look behind at what has stood the test of time, and to look around at what is working well now. Only then should one speculate on what is likely to work in the future. Over the centuries a fundamental bank of human wisdom on Organizational Capability has accumulated, which modern thought and experience can add to and expand. While I have avoided simply repackaging old ideas, I believe that this accumulated knowledge is worth restating and developing. To do this I have scoured my thirty years of academic research and consulting practice, as well as the ancient wisdom of the Western and Eastern worlds, and talked to colleagues and clients across five continents. Distinct patterns of effective organizing have emerged – ways of balancing and integrating tasks, social-emotional processes and learning which lead to a healthier balance of body, mind and spirit in both individuals and their organizations. These patterns transcend nationality, although the latter has a modifying effect on culturally bound organizations. I have tried to show those healthy mindsets, values and behaviours which I believe are necessary to create the para-doxically emotionally freer, and yet more self-disciplined, twenty-first-century organizations.

Fashionable novelty and cleverness do not give organizational wisdom, but many directors and managers are now so specialized that they can become easy prey for the latest business or management fashion outside their specialist field. By fixating on a specific fad or guru they can unwittingly reinforce the 'shadow side' of their organization, and so demean working life. Too often these specialists create organizational anorexia by trying to solve problems by slimming rapidly through fixated cost-cutting. Yet they can be prone simultaneously to organizational bulimia by binge-ing on any new business idea as it appears. They overdo it reck-lessly, then feel dreadful when the new wonder nostrum does not deliver as promised, so they throw up and start all over again.

In an attempt to avoid the worst excesses of corporate anorexia and bulimia I have kept in mind while I write a paragraph from the classic US novel *Angle of Repose* by Wallace Stegner:[2]

> I call the jury's attention to the way in which speculation has become supposition, supposition certainty, and certainty accusation. It's a lesson in the working of the expert mind, which can go from a hunch to an affidavit, and from an affidavit to a fee within minutes. With great authority the expert says what is not necessarily so.

The book is designed as a series of linked essays. There is some inevitable overlap. I hope that what repitition there is does not irritate the reader, indeed each essay is designed to be read on its own.

CHAPTER 1

The Business Case for Treating Organizations as Adaptive Learning Systems

Why do directors and managers design and operate organizations as if the people who comprise them do not matter? Why do they believe that people can be treated as cloned, interchangeable units in an impersonal machine? Why do they believe that there are no consequences from treating people this way? Why do they not play to the strengths of their most powerful and flexible resource – the energy and learning capacity of the people they employ?

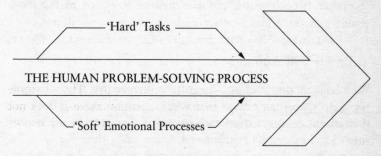

Figure 1 The human problem-solving process

It is rarely appreciated that organizing is a basic human building block which enables people to achieve more through co-operative problem-solving than any individual can achieve on their own. This 'soft', or human, aspect of organizational problem-solving cannot be separated from the 'hard', data-rational side of problem-resolution – the two aspects complement each other.

THE BASICS OF ORGANIZING

Organizing is made up of three fundamental building blocks:

- The achievement of tasks – the 'hard', rational, quantitative side of organizing
- The use of appropriate social processes to ensure the effective delivery of the task by releasing the emotional energy of the people involved – the 'soft', qualitative, side of organizing
- Learning regularly and rigorously from the total activity – the integrative, quantifiable, side of organizing

These three related elements are rarely appreciated by directors and managers, yet they form the basis of all effective organizations, because it is only by combining all three that good business results can be sustained. If hitting targets, creating a fulfilled workforce or satisfying customers is pursued to the exclusion of the other two elements, business will be damaged in the long term.

Training and Appraisal

An intelligent observer would naturally assume that those charged with giving organizations direction, energy and control are trained in ensuring Organizational Capability so that the necessary tasks and results are achieved. It should be their core skill. It is, but, sadly, they are usually untrained. At best, most directors and managers have acquired some rather random, uncodified experience. Such experience is often composed of a series of low-level compromises and mistakes which occurred during their working life. Rather than learn consciously from their mistakes, they often repeat the same error at each stage of their career.

In many cases the verb 'career' is apt here, because if managers have not pursued a single, specialist function during their working life then they are likely to have veered randomly from position to position often learning little – a form of organizational Brownian Motion. On the other hand, specialists or professionals are likely to repeat certain pre-ordered experiences year after year, with little critical review or appraisal. The usual priority is to churn out work, hit targets and deliver budgets, regardless of the consequences to the human side of the enterprise. For many engineers, lawyers, accountants, bankers and others in seemingly hard-edged disciplines, this is the only end for which they were trained.

Curiously, in most appraisal systems, directors and managers are over-assessed on the delivery of short-term business targets yet are only rarely assessed on their other organizational competences. The tyranny of annual budgets mean that achieving the 'hard', quantified, task is usually considered more than sufficient by most directors and general managers. They are comfortable to be measured on this alone, as they know how to play this type of micro-political game. The top management of one of my financial services clients says that they spend nearly ten months of the year fighting over budget allocations, and only two months focusing on delivering the service.

The achievement of task is necessary, but is not sufficient in itself for truly capable organizations. The consequences of not assessing the 'soft' aspects of organizing affect negatively both the short-term efficiency and the long-term effectiveness of any organization. We all live with the consequences every day in our dealings with demotivated, non-learning, non-adaptive and customer-unfriendly organizations. Initially the idea of measuring the 'soft' aspects of organizing can generate negative reactions, and can seem a thankless, even unnerving, job for directors and managers, but without it they will not have a capable organization to guide.

Natural Connections

If we go back to the meaning of words, the English verb 'to organize' comes from the Old French, meaning the connection and co-ordination of vital functions or processes. It entered the English

language in the fourteenth century relating to biological concepts, especially plants, and still retains a strong biological flavour
concerning living systems and forms. By the early nineteenth century the verb was being applied to both systems and groups of
people and the meaning evolved to: 'the action of putting into a
systematic whole with mutually connected and dependent parts'.[3]

Many people have either lost, or never had, the concept that
organizations are about human life forces, systematic connections
and mutual dependency. They are about living, complex and
adaptive systems. In the twentieth century the dominant tendency
was for writers and artists to portray them as the converse
– inhumane, unintegrated and divisive. This is a surprisingly
widespread perception, often reinforced through many negative
personal experiences, either as customers or as employees. We,
and organizations, are the worse for it.

Organizations are crucially important human institutions. They
form the basis of the private and public companies, public sector
agencies and non-profit associations of our society. The very
terms 'association' and 'company' are powerful reminders of the
human need to come together for mutual support, protection,
development and recognition. Indeed, the word 'company' originates in the idea of people coming together to break bread. We
organize so that by such coming together individual human beings
can satisfy two basic needs.

First, the social needs for continuation of the species, protection, association, status and, in Western societies, for ultimate
personal recognition. In Eastern societies recognition of the
family or work group tends to transcend that of the individual.
Second, the social economic need to create goods and services
which would be beyond the capacity of any single person to pro-
duce. In this way villages, towns, cities, companies, international
corporations, governments and voluntary organizations are
brought into being, grow, thrive and eventually die. Within these
bodies 'hard' tasks and 'soft' social processes combine to satisfy
both these social and economic needs. Human combination in
organizations allows for levels of specialization of work and
leisure which no individual could achieve alone.

Given that human beings have been organizing themselves into ever larger groups over the millennia, thus enabling the building of structures from Stonehenge, the pyramids, the buildings of Zimbabwe and the Great Wall of China, to the high-technologically led triumphs of the US and Russia's manned space exploration, and the creation of the global Internet, it would be reasonable to assume that we are good at it. We are not. We usually achieve our tasks at the expense of individuals and groups, after much misdirected, occasionally demeaning, effort.

The human race's natural tendency to group together for mutual benefit should, in theory, make us good at recognizing, and coping with, organizational incompetence, and should mean that Organizational Capability is the primary value sought in our leaders. Unfortunately this is not the case. Without an appropriate language and models to describe and quantify the issues it is hard to discuss the differences between what exists and what is needed in terms of achieving purpose through Organizational Capability: so natural human characteristics are frequently crushed by inappropriate organizational structures, processes and emotional climates. These are usually created unknowingly by the people at the top, so forcing many employees to exist against their better judgement in conditions which repeatedly show that they do not matter.

THE IMPORTANCE OF IMPROVING ORGANIZATIONAL CAPABILITY

People as a Valuable Resource

One of the great lies in business is the chairman's statement in the annual report that 'our people are our greatest asset'. If this is true, why are they not valued financially so that they appear on the balance sheet? In most organizations people tend to be counted only as a cost, not as an investment which will, in turn, create an asset. As a result, senior managers tend to treat people as economically suspect, and as something which should be reduced or cut out at any opportunity. This is very short-sighted, us of the three classic inputs to the business equation – land, labour and capital – only people are capable of adapting and learning. They are the only asset which can generate sufficient energy to drive the enterprise forwards, or to block it. The other two elements solely provide the context in which adapting and learning can occur.

Fortunately, as we reach the twenty-first century, some organizations are beginning to take the human input to Organizational Capability and effectiveness seriously, by treating it as an investment. They ensure that its assessment is given as high a priority as the financial measures, and that it is carried out regularly and rigorously. This is not a new phenomenon, and a growing number of studies show the beneficial effects of an organization ensuring that its people are valued. In his book *Beyond World Class*[4] Clive Morton quotes figures which make a compelling argument for giving 'soft' measures equal priority with the 'hard':

- Good people management practices can give twenty per cent productivity and profit improvement compared with six per cent from a combination of research and development, innovation and quality investment.
- Maintaining effective trust relationships and (voice) communication with suppliers and employees gives consistently higher productivity and profits.
- Agility of organizations is a function of a culture of learning and change within the organization – a speed of response going beyond quality, cost and delivery.
- Those companies that are 'inclusive' in both their internal and external relationships stay the course, are consistently more profitable, and better able to make strategic choices for the future.
- Those companies that exploit total quality systems to the full outperform the market place in every sense.
- Leading companies are those which live with ambiguity and deal effectively with dilemmas.

Morton's research and assertions are reinforced by a long-term study (1991–2001) by the London School of Economics and the University of Sheffield of over 100 UK, medium-sized, single-site manufacturing companies.[5] Amongst their interim findings are:

- Most companies fail to make the causal connection between good management practices and business success. The researchers state that 'this separation in the minds of senior managers between business and people management indicated that, for most, the rhetoric of employees being the most valuable resource, was often simply rhetoric'.
- Job satisfaction is thought to explain some sixteen per cent of the differences between, and the variations within, companies.
- Organizational commitment explains some seven per cent of the differences between, and variations within, companies.
- A noticeable twenty-nine per cent variation in productivity between companies was linked to the organization's culture, with concern for the employees' welfare playing a significant part.
- Good human resources practices explains nineteen per cent of the variations in profitability, and eighteen per cent of the variations in productivity over time.
- There is a causal connection between good people management and sustained company performance, through such key factors as job design, flexibility of and responsibility for jobs, especially at the shopfloor level, and the acquisition and development of skills via good selection, induction, training and appraisal.
- In terms of management practices previously thought to affect company performance such as business strategy, emphasis on quality, use of advanced manufacturing technology and investment in research and development, it was surprising to find that only research and development influenced profitability, where it accounted for eight per cent of the variation.

The authors concluded 'that if managers wish to influence the performance of their companies, the most important area they should emphasize is the management of people. This is ironic, given that our research also demonstrated that emphasis on human resource management is one of the most neglected areas of management practice within organizations.'

This powerful evidence should lead directors and senior managers to take the human side of organization seriously. It is a wise investment for them to ensure that people management is given as much care and maintenance as any of the 'hard' aspects of the organization. The feedback from these 'people' systems, the learning of the organization through this investment, needs to be treated as rigorously as their financial budgets.

Assessment

How can this be done? First, by ensuring that the day-to-day Operational Learning is collected and reflected upon regularly to ensure a continuing process of improvement to service delivery, customer satisfaction, staff satisfaction, product and service quality and managerial systems. Second, directors and managers should study carefully and regularly this Operational Learning to create, at a strategic level, new assets for their organization – all 'intellectual property' resulting from their investment, over which a legal right can be established to create an asset, will eventually appear on the balance sheet.

Usable formulae which make manifest the business case for the more sympathetic use of human beings are currently being created. A fascinating study co-ordinated by Nigel Habershon for the European Foundation for Management Development[6] looks at the return on investment in training and development. Ten participating companies: including GE, IBM, Repsoil and BCH, and a shadow group consisting of Daimler Benz, Coca-Cola, ABN Amro Bank, GM, Lufthansa and Pirelli, have been working co-operatively to derive the new formulae.

Using material from Personal Decisions International (PDI) they are trying to move from a traditional financial model to a new model which includes the human element.

Now that such powerful companies are co-operating in the

Traditional Financial Model

$$\frac{\text{Profits}}{\text{Equity}} = \frac{\text{Profits}}{\text{Sales}} \times \frac{\text{Sales}}{\text{Assets}} \times \frac{\text{Assets}}{\text{Equity}}$$

ROE   Margin   Productivity   Leverage

Where is HR? An expense which reduces profits . . .

Traditional HR measures:
- % of sales
- HR to Total Headcount Ratio
- Training Cost per Person

New Financial Model

It's no longer how does 'money make money'? but how does intellectual capital make money?

$$\frac{\text{Profits}}{\text{Sales}} = \frac{\text{Organizational Investments}}{\text{Sales}} \times \frac{\text{Capabilities}}{\text{Organizational Investments}} \times \frac{\text{Profits}}{\text{Capabilities}}$$

ROE =   Investment × Effectiveness × Impact
          (Finance)   (HR)   (Finance *and* HRD)

Model for relating HR investments to profits

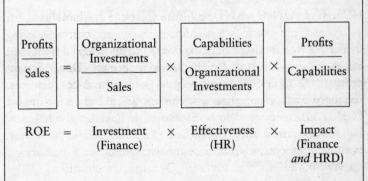

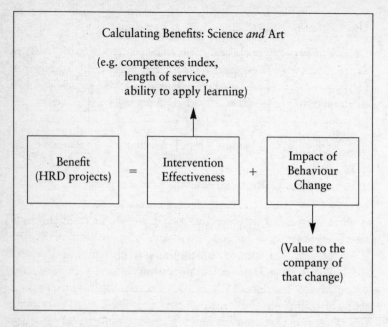

Calculating Benefits: Science *and* Art

(e.g. competences index,
length of service,
ability to apply learning)

Benefit (HRD projects) = Intervention Effectiveness + Impact of Behaviour Change

(Value to the company of that change)

expectation of creating a major return on a cost-effective, modest investment the business case for treating people as crucial components of a living organization is finally being made effectively.

OPERATIONAL AND STRATEGIC LEARNING

There are two levels of organizational learning, Operational and Strategic, co-ordinated by the learning board situated at the centre of a figure-of-eight (see p. 63). The strategic drive for organizational effectiveness and the operational drive for organizational efficiency need to be continuously linked and rebalanced by the directors and executives. Learning how to achieve both simultaneously needs a strong awareness of Organizational Capability.

Operational Learning

During day-to-day operations every line manager, at all levels of the organization, from supervisor to chairman, needs to ask four fundamental questions at the beginning or end of each piece of work, whether this comprises a shift, a day or a week:

1 What went right?
2 What went wrong?
3 What can we do about it?
4 Who else needs to know?

At first sight this may seem prosaic. It is not. Such 'intelligently naive' questioning is *the* basic work discipline for line managers. It is very powerful, as it both drives internal efficiency and focuses thinking, effort and actions on the best responses to changing customer needs. The regular use of such questioning, and the actions that derive from it, will create in the customer's mind over time, the perception that your products or services offer good value for money.

In business terms it is vital to avoid falling victim to the 'big C' – 'commoditization'. Unless you are the cost-leader in your field, then once infected by commoditization you are trapped in a vicious cycle of decline because customers cannot differentiate you from any other supplier, so you compete only on lowest price. So unless you are the cost-leader in your field then you are on the downward path to corporate collapse.

How does such a 'hard' notion fit with the idea of accentuating people and emotions in organizations? Many business people accept that there is a strong causal relationship between the two. In *Brand Warriors*[7] Fiona Gilmore makes the point that brands have two elements to them. First, there are the tangible ('hard') benefits which visibly differentiate them from their competitors. Even in seemingly commoditized sectors like blue jeans and supermarkets, much can be made of these. Second, there are the intangible ('soft') benefits. These give people a positive, warm feeling about using the product or service, and create a good feeling about being associated with it. The convergence of these two emotions develops brand loyalty to the product, or service, which gives distinct economic advantages in terms of customer retention, and the willingness to pay a premium price, which the customers themselves may not be able to explain in terms of economic rationality.

The retention of good customers is a key business success factor. 'Good' customers pay on time, appreciate your offering, pay a price premium, remain loyal and reduce noticeably your cost of sales. They seek you out, rather than the reverse, and do not need a heavy advertising spend to convince them of the benefits of your offering. Because they are already convinced, they are less likely to swap to competitors unless they are offered overwhelming advantages, and even then, the emotional benefits will make it hard for them to leave. At one end of the scale are the shoppers who can differentiate quite distinct and subtle advantages of always shopping at, say, a Tesco or Sainsburys supermarket. At the other end are those who are wedded to flying first class with Cathay Pacific or British Airways.

The retention of good customers is crucially dependent on the retention of good, experienced staff. It is hardly surprising that brand loyalty begins to suffer if service levels are cut, small perceived customer benefits are abolished, and the 'emotional contract' between the customer and the company is often broken, either thoughtlessly or even unwittingly. This process is rationalized by senior executives as improving the 'bottom line' and, therefore, 'increasing shareholder value'. One can always improve a bottom line in the short term, but cannot necessarily achieve the expected increase in shareholder value.

The leadership issue for the directors and executives is whether continuous downsizing can be done in the medium and long term. Will over-focusing on cost-reduction alone destroy the customer base? It will if the directors see the main micro-economic levers of the business only as the operational relationships between volume, cost and price, and then pull consistently on the Cost lever in the hope of improving profitability. This is not a viable business strategy, and is not wise in the long term. Nor is it a sustainable method of delivering shareholder value.

The main problem with a tactic based solely on cost-reduction is that it upsets loyal customers, who quickly notice the breaking of their previous emotional contract through the 'improvement' or 'simplification' of the product or service features they valued previously, and which differentiated you from your competitors. This includes elements such as the loss of face-to-face, or voice-to-voice, time at the bank, small presents or services on airlines and the more mechanical processing of patients at doctors' surgeries. In the absence of such features customers quickly become more fickle and prone to switch to competitors. This makes your cost of sales rise sharply as you fight to get them back or, worst of all, have to go to the expense of generating significant numbers of new customers. Many organizations make this mistake time after time. They do not have the learning systems in place that would enable them to rectify this fundamental economic problem, and to understand that people do matter – both customers and staff.

They are like the Bourbon kings – compelled to learn nothing and forget nothing – and so to underperform the market. Again, cost-fixated behaviour is justified by many executives as being caused by the 'necessary tyranny of the annual budget'. This is usually followed by the 'it's more than my job's worth to make changes around here' argument. Both these rationales reflect Tom Peters' famous demolition of the 'vision' of an hotel chain who cried in anguish that they 'were no worse than any other hotel chain'. He asked, rightly, what motivational effect this had on staff and customers? What sort of emotional contract is that? Good staff properly selected, trained and developed, dealing face-to-face in real time with individual consumers, are much more likely to retain good customers. They are relatively expensive if viewed only as a simple unit cost, but in terms of cost-effectiveness they are a key investment.

So, it is hard to see how long-term shareholder value can be increased without long-term customer satisfaction, yet far too many companies behave as if there is no causal link between the two. They argue that improving the bottom line, even at unrealistically short, quarterly, intervals, is an inviolable demand from their shareholders, especially the fund managers, who will other-wise sell their shares immediately. This is untrue. The 1997 National Association of Pension Funds statistics show that UK fund managers tend to hold their shares on average for seven years. They tend not to trade on the margin. Who is trying to fool who here? It is truer to say that following an unimaginative, lemming-like formula, and downsizing without rigorous analysis of its total effects causes decline, as breaking the emotional con-tract signals the time when loyal customers leave in search of something even marginally better than the cost-cuting offering. If the organization lacks sufficient Organizational Capability to respond, then it is quickly in real trouble.

In his book *Corporate Amnesia*[8] Arnold Kransdorff develops the idea of 'organizational memory'. He argues that with an increasingly flexible labour market replacing many organizations' total workforces every five years, organizations are forfeiting their know-how and know-why faster than they can replace it. Organi-zational memory consists of the knowledge, attitudes and skills accrued from the unique experiences of the people comprising the organization at any one time. It is an effect of the organization's investment in its intellectual assets, and the key to its durability. If an organization has the ability to pass on such collective memory, then it has a major competitive advantage, and without that abil-ity the organization cannot benefit from its own hindsight and experiences. This helps to explain why so many productivity improvement plans are so difficult to deliver – people's learn-ing is not continuously codified and turned into Organizational Capability.

Strategic Learning

While Operational Learning directly affects the profit-and-loss account, Strategic Learning affects the balance sheet. It re-quires that directors get into 'intellectual helicopter' mode to rise above day-to-day problems, and search for patterns in the chang-ing external environment which allow them to understand the changing competitive pressures, ensure that they have the Organizational Capabilities to handle them, and to create new assets, especially intellectual property rights, which will be reflected on the balance sheet.

People learn every day as they live and work in the external environment surrounding their organization, and this learning can inform and energize the board's drive for organizational effectiveness. Sadly, the business problem is that sufficient attention is rarely paid to this investment. The necessity of learning at the strategic level is not specified in the job descriptions and appraisal systems of directors and executives, and they do not take the time to reflect on the organizational patterns of capabilities and organizational memory, which flow from the results.

Even worse, they often create an emotional climate in an organization where people will not share their learning, either because strategic information gives them organizational power, or because they are frightened to admit a mistake. Lines of communication then become blocked, energy is diverted to hiding mistakes, and people will not speak their minds, even when they know what is wrong. At its very worst the emotional climate can become so poisoned that people lie systematically and 'malicious obedience' takes over – people obey orders explicitly even when they know that the wrong outcomes will occur. When, as frequently happens, this occurs during the implementation of strategies, then the organization is in trouble.

I came across a good example of a negative emotional climate in Zimbabwe recently, where a simple system had been installed in a big bakery to stop large numbers of loaves from being burnt inadvertently. A worker had been told to watch the bread, and a lever had been installed for him to pull if he saw it burning. However, his supervisor also told him never to use the lever without consulting him. The bread frequently came close to burning but, as the supervisor was rarely to be found, the worker did not pull the lever, and let the bread burn. The wastage rate remained high, despite the avowed intention of lowering it.

It is the responsibility of directors and managers to create and maintain a positive climate for continuous learning in their organization. They have a further duty to ensure the creation and protection of the asset base of their organization. While they are often comfortable with dealing with assets such as property, retained profits, shareholders' funds etc., the idea that the outcome of their learning, and the generation of intellectual property, should be added to the balance sheet can be shocking to them.

Yet, as the speed of change increases in the external environment, the only resource that can ensure that the rate of learning is equal to, or greater than, the rate of change is your people – your Organizational Capability.

INTELLECTUAL PROPERTY

I stress again that learning is not just an operational issue concerning the day-to-day workings of the organization. It is also concerned with the creation and protection of 'knowledge assets'. Max Boisot, in *Knowledge Assets: Securing Competitive Advantage in the Information Economy*,[9] says:

> we are only just beginning to think of knowledge assets as economic goods in their own right. Thinking of knowledge in this way is turning out to be more challenging than might be supposed, since there is a natural tendency to assimilate what is unknown to what is known. The early automobiles, for example, were known as 'horseless carriages'. In order to gain acceptance, they had to have, as far as possible, the 'look and feel' of a horse-drawn vehicle. So it is with information goods. In order to be accepted as such, an information good is expected to have the look and feel of a physical good. Unfortunately, the look and feel of knowledge assets are anything but physical.
> A failure to properly conceptualize the nature of knowledge assets, however, condemns firms – and indeed whole economies – to fight tomorrow's competitive battles with yesterday's outdated weapons and tactics.

One approach to harnessing the power of Strategic Learning is to have systematic audits throughout the organization every few months, to check which ideas, systems, products or services have been developed recently, and over which intellectual property rights can be created. The basic structure of intellectual property was clearly defined through the World Trade Organization in 1995 and consists of:

Patent
Copyright
Registered design
Trademark
Servicemark

In some countries trade secrets and moral ownership can be added.

All of these are assets which can be valued and placed on a balance sheet. We are not talking small numbers here. Whole industries rise on them – pharmaceuticals are driven by the search for patents. Computer software has been driven by the search for copyright, although some recent US cases suggest that patents might be given for software too. The rise and rise of Microsoft to become a predominant world corporation within a decade is a prime example of this. Bill Gates had software rights valued at US$11.56 billion in 1998. Hans Rausing, the inventor and developer of Tetrapak cartons, now has family assets of around £3 billion. Any music, book or software publisher can be sitting on a potential fortune, as can engineers, architects, lawyers, and sports and film stars.

The latter are increasingly buying the rights to their films and using their existing intellectual property to raise money for other projects. David Bowie recently raised £35 million by using the rights from his music portfolio as security, and Nicole Kidman followed a similar strategy in her purchase of the film rights to *In the Cut*. Then there are the merchandising rights associated with success, particularly in the field of football. Arsenal, like so many top clubs, makes significant profits out of its sale of its strip and associated memorabilia. Jacques Villeneuve, the Formula One driver, is trying to register his face as a trademark for a global merchandising venture.

This may still sound like a crazy new world to many directors and managers, but they should reflect on the fact that whereas in the old world of 'tangible assets' capital tended to be focused on 'hard' things, thereby reinforcing the concept that people are add-ons to machines, in the 'intangible asset' world of intellectual property a 'soft' approach is essential, because increasingly, staff are their own tools.

This is a key point. The new attitudes, knowledge and skills needed by directors and managers to cope with business survival and growth in the new knowledge-intensive industries lie in the 'soft' competences of creating the tasks and emotional climate which release and then use organizational learning. This means releasing from the people in whom you have invested the knowledge, attitudes and skills that lead to the know-how and know-why which in turn creates patents and registered designs; releasing the imagination, creativity and innovation that creates copyright, and releasing the exploitative marketing nous that creates brands, trademarks and servicemarks. This is true Strategic Learning.

To thoughtlessly downsize is to waste assets which may, at the worst, walk out and find jobs with your competitors.

CHAPTER 2

Obstacles to Creating Capable Organizations

The biggest obstacle to creating capable organizations is the belief held by many directors, managers and staff that organizations must be, by definition, mechanical, inhumane, nasty and brutish if they are to be efficient. This warped mindset is often found in the teachings of accountancy and management, either explicitly or implicitly. The challenge, in terms of developing Organizational Capability, is to change this mindset and create a recognition that organizations are key *human* institutions – networks of people working towards a common purpose through systems and a culture which all have helped to create, and which continues to evolve. If this can be achieved, then even bureaucracy has its rightful place as an option in the range of human institutions. Unfortunately, an emotionally negative form of bureaucracy is often seen as the only choice.

APPROPRIATE BUREAUCRACY

All organizations are, in part, a human response to uncertainty. One of the social triumphs of the bloody and turbulent twentieth century has been the reduction of much uncertainty through the development of large-scale organizational bureaucracies. These have enabled huge numbers of people to work within precisely defined rules of what they can, and cannot, do to administer massive organizations, and to take consistent decisions. There are strict sanctions in these bureaucracies if you go outside your job authority levels, and tightly predetermined mechanisms for moving difficult choices beyond each level upwards to a final decision point. Such bureaucracies have helped reduce chaos in many societies by providing stability and certainty – at a price. Bureaucracies can be highly inflexible, and in fast-changing times they have received an increasingly bad press.

However, when a high degree of certainty, control, and precision is demanded in the work processes, e.g. in the engineering division of an airline, or the control room of a nuclear power station, or in a hospital's operating theatre, bureaucracies are a necessity (see p. 46). Readers will think of highly publicized film examples such as *Airplane, The Simpsons* and *MASH* to disprove my point. I counter with the thought that it is the powerful contradiction between our experience and aspirations, and the anarchy of these satires that gives each its biting humour. We know what should happen and have a fearful laugh at the resulting antics. They are very funny, yet they also reinforce the cynical, negative image of formal organizations in the public's mind.

Sadly bureaucracies are now often stereotyped as mindless and heartless machines, devoid of passion, justice or even hope for those employed within them. But they are just one of a range of organizational forms – from the power-centred chaos of Robert Maxwell's empire to the totally people-centred collegiality of Rumpole of the Bailey's chambers – which directors and managers can select, as appropriate. Why do so many people cling to the outdated stereotype that there is only one formal organizational type, the bureaucracy, and that all bureaucracies are bad?

The Faustian Employment Contract

One simple answer is that in the modern world of work many believe that to survive they must keep obeying orders from an impersonal bureaucratic machine, regardless of the consequences. Thus, many people will bend their principles, values and behaviour to obey doubtful orders. Cynics will say that this is part of the human condition. The more academic of them will quote the classic Milgram studies[10] on 'yielding' to back their claims – the vast majority of people, when faced with an authority figure giving illegal orders in a tough and threatening manner, will yield to those orders, regardless of the personal stress that puts the individual through.

This is damaging for society. People will question doubtful orders if the emotional climate of the organization encourages constructive critical review by humans of humans, but this is less likely to happen if they have only one, bureaucratic and impersonal model in their vocabulary of organizational structure and capability. This 'one club' approach to organizing is patently ineffective in a rapidly changing world, yet it has developed an apparent legal backing over the last two centuries through the creation and widespread use of the contract of personal employment. The vast majority of us offer ourselves to an organization which will pay us for supplying our labour, skills and knowledge for a specified amount of time each week. There is nothing wrong with the process of contracting our labour, indeed, our society is built on it and, despite the present trends towards redefining employment contracts into smaller, more diffuse and lower-cost units, the full-time employment contract is still predominant throughout the world. However, it is worth nothing that in the UK in 1998 full-time paid employment dropped to just thirty-nine per cent of the working population, and continues to fall.

As the world of work becomes less predictable people can easily be pushed by directors and managers to abandon their aspirations to achieve higher levels of status and self-esteem in organizations and to slide into fear, depression and the need for protection at any price. They believe, wrongly, that doing anything an organization asks of them will guarantee its continuing protection of themselves and their families. This is the 'I was only obeying orders' defence. In the short term this can be made by managers to appear entirely rational. In the medium to long term it is cancerous to healthy organizational thinking, learning and behaviour. If people do not review critically what is occurring, speak their minds, and share their learning, then problems will grow. These are the very conditions which will inevitably lead to decline.

There are shadow sides to any organization, where real behaviours bear no relationship to the espoused values. People are rarely asked to adopt truly inhumane values and actions, as the erosion of personal and group values is usually more subtle. This forms a classic dilemma for an individual in an organization – how do you keep your personal integrity when the organization's demands run counter to it? How do you strike a balance between the two horns of this age-old dilemma? On one side the organization's demands are weighted with the rewards of obeying unquestioningly and the consequences of disobeying. On the other side is the question of what your conscience will allow you to do. People have beliefs, values and behaviours which keep them sane, healthy and able to live with themselves. Increasingly impersonal organizational demands for only 'hard' task achievement through less and less effective 'soft' social-emotional processes, causes stress and tension within individuals, and within and between work groups. This is often rationalized by the individual saying 'Well, I don't agree with this but I will do it just this once to protect myself,' until the action becomes such a corrosive habit that they reach a crisis point where they lose their social intelligence and working humanity.

When social process is absent effective task achievement will not occur, eventually leading to the collapse of the organization. A good example is demonstrated through the well-known 'Abilene Paradox', where a group takes a decision which if you question them later, each individual member feels, or knows, is wrong, but where the lack of sufficient social process within the group discouraged critical review or debate.

It needs to be recognized that the contract of employment has both an economic/legal and an emotional element to it. Yes, we want the job, the rewards and the guarantee of employment, but there is more to it than that – the organization is also buying *me* and all I stand for. The latter element is rarely discussed, let alone emotionally contracted, during the selection or induction processes of a job, or checked during regular appraisal. Yet it is the very basis of the effective induction and inclusion of an employee into a work group and, especially, of the building of a healthy working relationship. It is every line manager's job to do this. Unless induction and inclusion are handled by each line manager in this way it is very difficult for an individual to become truly competent in their specific job.

Some forward-thinking organizations are beginning to recognize that the old employment contract is a Faustian deal, whereby people effectively offer their soul in return for the guarantee of life-long employment. These organizations know that they can no longer offer that. Gone are the days when a global bank would select its international staff at the age of twenty-one and retire them at fifty-two, rich and mentally and physically exhausted. In the years between they were on twenty-four hours' notice to work full-time anywhere in the world the bank chose to send them. Their families would follow, unquestioningly, as soon as possible after the transfer.

What is beginning to be on offer, especially in 'knowledge worker' companies, like multi-media design, corporate counselling, investment banking and now even retail banking, is the idea of the employment contract 'ensuring *employability*'. The contract still spells out the 'hard' side of tasks to be achieved, basic pay, hours, conditions etc., but it is honest enough to also include the 'soft' side, guaranteeing that, while the length of employment is for a short term, typically two to four years during which time all the usual benefits apply, the emotional side of the contract is to aspire to keep them longer and to promise to give sufficient training and personal development within the duration of the contract, via agreed time and money budgets, so that the individual has a high chance of retaining their employability on the wider labour market. This is ascertained through careful and regular appraisal between the individual and their boss. Early signs are that this is proving a highly cost-effective way of recruiting, developing and retaining well-qualified staff, and of ensuring their commitment until the moment they have to leave.

The widespread failure to understand the social-emotional aspects of employment contracts generates two key blockages to Organizational Capability. First, large amounts of human energy, experience, creativity and potential are lost to an organization when the emotional balance of an employment contract is disturbed – when the employee's 'perception of equity' is lost. People become demotivated, prone to making mistakes or to not following instructions, tempted into 'malicious obedience' and, at worst, to organizational sabotage. Second, the implied assumption that the employment contract is merely economic indicates that in the normal process of being contracted employees must lose the majority of their unique human characteristics, and play down their feelings and their learning. They are forced to become an impersonal part of an impersonal whole.

Both are dangerous mindsets for organizations and individuals. They allow the people in power, without critical review, to focus solely on the 'hard' achievement of task by any means they deem fit, at the expense of the 'soft' social process and, therefore, the cohesion of the whole. This blocks organizational learning and turns the focus away from co-operative learning and towards individual learning blaming others and personal survival.

The Vocabulary of Organizing

I have no wish to try and return to a romanticized organizational Arcadian dawn, where people group naturally together around stable-state, agrarian communities based on egalitarian lines chanting 'When Adam delved and Eve span who was then the gentleman?' Such notions, dear to William Morris and his followers, are impossible to achieve if one wishes to survive in the era of mass consumerism, global communications and global trade systems. So, barring Armageddon, we are faced with making the best of our existing organizations. It is up to you and me to ensure that we do. We must strive to rebalance organizational tasks and processes in favour of the 'soft', social-emotional side, and to do that we have to confront a number of deep-rooted stereotypes which have formed the basis of our thinking about organizations for at least the last two centuries. We need to develop a vocabulary of Organizational Capability which eradicates these assumptions.

THE BELIEF THAT PEOPLE ARE NATURALLY LAZY

First is the powerful directoral and managerial belief that people are inherently untrustworthy, lazy and activated only by rational economic need – they will do as little as they can for the money offered. Given the negative emotional climates in many organizations, this may well be a rational response from employees to an irrational set of beliefs and demands from their employers. The danger is that this becomes a self-fulfilling prophecy. People treated as lazy and untrustworthy will over time behave that way. This is not because they are inherently unreliable, but rather because they have a deep human need for recognition from others which is being fulfilled negatively. People find it very hard to face a condition where they receive no personal recognition, whether from their family, work group, friends or people in power.

If there is no positive recognition built into their appraisal, both through financial and non-financial rewards, like thanks and praise, then, rather than have no recognition at all, they will seek negative recognition. They will knowingly make mistakes, and work slowly and badly so that they will be shouted at, criticized and punished. This is not the best type of personal recognition but it is preferable to being ignored totally. Such a negative emotional climate pushes people into a vicious downwards spiral which can incapacitate an organization. People will hide mistakes, blame others, cover up, then cover up the cover up, and spend most of their energy on activities unrelated to achieving the task in hand.

By doing so, they cannot learn regularly and rigorously from their work – this applies throughout an organization. People block their lines of communication, reducing their ability to handle the positive aspects of task and social process and thereby preventing the development of healthy, effective and efficient organizations. Organizational incapability is often an understandable reaction to the negative attitudes of directors and managers who have condemned staff to spend their work lives in a vicious, non-learning cycle. When attempting to create capable organizations it is essential to ensure that directors and managers live out their rhetoric that 'our people are our biggest asset'. It has been shown in many studies that if a teacher is told that some pupils are above average and others below, then they treat them in that way and the exam results reflect this. Similarly, if managers behave in a way that shows them to believe that their direct reports are intelligent, energetic, take pride in their work, and are above all, human, then the typical vicious circle of organizational life can be turned into a virtuous circle.

ORGANIZATIONS AS MACHINES

The second debilitating stereotype is that organizations are essentially machines. This is patently absurd, and yet it is deeply held by many people in power. It has become entrenched through such modern folk stories as Charlie Chaplin's *Modern Times* (the small man against the robber barons of capitalism), *Dilbert*[11] (the extraordinarily popular cartoon series detailing the incompetence and incomprehensibility of modern managers, management consultants and human resource directors) and Franz Kafka's *The Trial* and *The Castle* (the individual against the psychic prison of unfeeling bureaucracy). The latter is very important to European and US thinking about organizations, as it not only depicts remorseless bureaucracy as a soulless machine, but also as a psychic prison from which it is impossible to escape. The idea of the helpless individual, employee and victim, trapped in a never-ending bureaucratic nightmare is a very powerful twentieth-century mindset which needs changing if we are to achieve healthy twenty-first-century organizations.

Why is the image of the employee-as-victim so powerful? One answer is that we fool ourselves into believing that such a concept must be true if everyone repeats it enough. For example, we have a great belief in the importance and efficacy of 'organization charts' or 'organograms'. We draw organization charts to explain to ourselves and others the current functions and hierarchies to 'show how the organization works'. Divisions, units and work groups have symmetrical lines drawn between them to reinforce the hierarchies. These are patently untrue. Go into any organization armed with its formal organization chart and compare it to what is actually happening informally. At the most prosaic level some people will be away – ill, on holiday, at a conference, or being trained. Some positions will be vacant because they are still seeking candidates or just cannot get them, or there has been a freeze on recruitment. Some jobs, or even whole departments, will have been disbanded through euphemistically termed 'lean and mean' cutbacks. On any one day it is simply not the organization as shown in the chart. Yet it still works informally with a degree of effectiveness and efficiency.

This is because the people who comprise it want it to. They do not buy the impersonal, machine model of organizations, and act out their belief that their organization is a living, complex, adaptive organism. The organization is where they get their protection, association, status, recognition, self-esteem and pay. Their reasons may be of the highest moral and ethical level, as seen in Quaker, Amish, kibbutzim, Islamic or Buddhist communities, or they may be of the lowest and most venal – the important fact is that they fulfil most of their needs through this organization. It sustains them, and in the best cases nurtures and develops them. It also demands a lot from them.

It has often been argued that organizations are about achieving tasks and nurturing people, particularly since the research work of the Tavistock Institute, London identified the concept of the 'socio-technical' systems in 1947. This is necessary but not sufficient, as it still allows a binary, 'either . . . or' view to be too readily accepted. In the current, bottom-line oriented climate such a view will inevitably tilt the balance of an organization in the direction of task fixation. I want to see organizations agreeing that they can only achieve tasks through nurturing and developing people – staff, customers, suppliers, directors, managers and local communities – rather than viewing people as the major obstacles to task achievement.

There is solid business evidence to support the theory that a positive emotional climate allows fewer mistakes, and nurtures learning, effectiveness, efficiency, customer satisfaction and supply-chain relationships, so creating greater shareholder value and longer-lasting organizations.

The business value of a positive, people-orientated approach can be clearly seen, for example, in programmes designed to reduce mistakes and accidents. The UK's Health and Safety Executive says that each year the UK loses 33 million working days through work-related accidents and illness at a cost to the economy of £16 billion. The average direct cost to business is £200 for every employee per year, excluding the cost of damage to the business's reputation, and of reprocessing lost orders. By focusing on action learning processes amongst its staff Unipart plc cut its accident costs by £300,000 in 1996, United Biscuits cut its insurance costs by 20 per cent in two years and saw a massive 60 per cent drop in employer's liability claims, compared to a national average increase of 20 per cent, and Norfolk Mental Health Care Trust implemented a new safety management programme and cut its annual insurance costs by 10 per cent. These figures reflect the definitive work on safety in coal mines by Reg Revans which demonstrated the power of self-help, multi-disciplined, action learning groups amongst the miners. His studies were carried out from 1947 onwards, and are prize examples of applied research, underpinned by good mathematics, affecting immediately people's working lives. It is a sad comment on our times that they have rarely been publicized.

Creating a positive emotional climate from the top is the antidote to the poisonous tendency to improve short-term bottom-line results to the long-term detriment of the total organization – what Charles Hampden-Turner so aptly referred to as 'the wet dreams of the rearguard of Western imperialism'. Yet the belief is still prevalent that organizations are machines to be tinkered with, and the people can be fitted in later – the Lego approach to organizational theory and practice.

THE TYRANNY OF SPECIALIZATION

Why do we persist with the notion of the organization as a machine? Francis Duffy, in his book *The New Office*,[12] blames much of the misery of modern organizational life on our over-reliance, particularly in business-school teaching, on the early twentieth-century research of F. W. Taylor. Taylor's detailed studies were on increasing work efficiency by breaking work into ever-smaller, more specialized, measurable units. This deskilled manufacturing work and, as long as the worker was treated as purely an impersonal and individual element of production, achieved remarkable results. In the world of manufacturing, this approach, at a time when large, unskilled pools of labour were available, was definitely a massive economic leap forward. However, it was not a positive social leap, and we are still suffering the consequences. 'Taylorism' is still being applied thoughtlessly to work which is increasingly interconnected, and where, when they are knowledge workers, the staff themselves are their own tools. Duffy remarks: 'The Taylorism-of-old may never have been much loved but it has certainly proved itself to be remarkably persistent.'

Take a trip around most medium- and large-scale offices to look at the organization and energy levels of the folk there. Then look at any of the wonderful *Dilbert* cartoons of Scott Adams to see the real motivators of people stuck in an open-plan office 'environment' trying to seek meaning in a web of apparently arbitrary decisions, personal values distorted to yield to fit them and management fads. Sadly, Dilbert has not chronicled the consequences of early unfettered Thatcherism in the UK but I am sure that the results are similar, and that we now have to rebalance our approach, especially before it infects too deeply the public sector ethos of government, local authorities, agencies and parastatals.

I believe that many of these problems are due to the process of increasing specialization by breaking work into smaller and dumber units. Specialization has undoubted massive advantages in allowing the more effective and efficient generation of products and services, but it has major disadvantages if taken to the extreme.

If a director's or senior manager's career has progressed only through specialized functions then it leaves them with little ability to see the organization as a whole, living, complex adaptive system. Specialization is the opposite of the word 'organization'. Typically, specialists are not encouraged to work across

organizational boundaries, nor can they usually imagine or understand the subtleties of the integration of the total organization.

The situation is often made worse by modern academic and
professional education processes which encourage specialization
rather than integration. These usually reward convergent thinking
styles above all else (focusing on finding 'the answer' while stripping out all apparently irrelevant information), and discourage
the exploration of diversity and the creative use of ambiguity and
differences. Yet such divergent and creative thinking is of increasing importance in rebalancing over-rational thinking in a chaotic
world. The ability to balance divergent and convergent thinking is
the essence of good design, whether of organizations, architecture
or products, but it is so alien to the education and experience of
the vast majority of directors and managers that it is unsurprising
that they cannot design holistic organization structures and
processes. This is a major cause of their preference for simple,
hierarchical and unreal organization charts.

Over-emphasis on specialization, and the consequent under-
emphasis on integration, also strongly affects the power structures
of the organization. It means that individuals and groups are
much more susceptible to divide-and-rule behaviours from senior
members of the organization. If the boundaries between groups,
both vertical and horizontal, are sharply demarcated and tightly
policed, then power resides in those who draw the lines, and those
who create and pass information around the organization. These
are the directors and managers of the formal organization and the
messengers, personal assistants, post-room assistants and tea
ladies servicing the informal organization (see p. 169). In government and business it is well known that some of the best sources
of information are chauffeurs. They overhear all sorts of informal
discussions and power-plays, and are often willing to talk about
them to demonstrate just how near the sources of power they are.

In the formal organization the message-passers have a vested
interest in ensuring that they tighten the inter-group boundaries,
thus increasing their usefulness, particularly if their jobs are under
threat. In these increasingly unpredictable times it is rational to
assume that the direction-givers would want to break down such

barriers to increase the flow of information and the number of possible connections – the organizational capability – to cope with rising work demands and decreased resources, but organizations are not necessarily run in a rational manner despite the rhetoric.

The present passion for the dis-integration, or dumbing-down, of meaningful jobs has been reinforced by financial pressures – the 'deskilling' of labour. This is the reduction of any job to its simplest and cheapest activities, so that the lowest cost-per-job can be had. This affects activities as diverse as making hamburgers, handling bank accounts, manufacturing cars, flying airliners or practising medicine or law. It seems a paradox that while we are frequently told that the twenty-first century will be The Information Age, filled with knowledge workers developing and protecting intellectual property as the main asset of their business, the main directoral and managerial behaviours seem to be stripping out the very attitudes, knowledge and skills needed for learning the holistic approaches involved in running such organizations. We seem keener to embed such learning in slivers of silicon rather than people.

At present, the near-sighted objective of many directors and senior managers seems to be to replace integrative human work with simple, repetitive, pre-determined behaviours which will quickly become machine-like, thoughtless habits. This cuts out the time-consuming and expensive process whereby staff gain experience. It is hardly surprising that many employed people feel like a cog in a machine – this is increasingly the reality, even if they are an airline captain or a board director. When treated like automata it is hardly surprising that people rebel, redirecting their energy towards winning small victories by baffling or subverting 'the machine'. Or they can break down irretrievably, because they cannot cope with the paradox that their experience and learning are seemingly valued at zero by the organization, and increasingly highly by customers.

Yet most directors and managers slog on, dutifully trying to achieve their tasks ever more efficiently with fewer and fewer resources and ever-expanding targets. Raising their eyes to the horizon, even if only occasionally, would show that there comes a point where increasing organizational efficiency seriously affects the customer's perception of organizational effectiveness. Either corporate amnesia sets in and they forget, or they have never realized, that, from the customer's point of view, the only thing that matters is perceived organizational effectiveness. That is what they pay for. Organizational efficiency is not a customer's problem.

CLEARING THE WAY FOR ORGANIZATIONAL CAPABILITY

There are signs of hope on the horizon. Cynics will claim that this is is a false dawn but I doubt this for four reasons. First, because customers are increasingly revolting against the iniquitous consequences of thoughtless downsizing. Many companies, especially banks, have cut costs by stripping out their 'back offices' and centring them in regional or national processing centres. So far so good. However, they then take this rationalizing logic too far for a service industry by applying unimaginative and unemotional thought process to the customers' 'moments of truth' – the point where they meet or talk with a member of staff. 'Service centres' are created which promise more, but then paradoxically give much reduced or minimal service. Being centralized, young and inexperienced, but cheap, the staff are unskilled at coping with individual customer needs, and they block the customer's ability to contact their local bank directly because all telephone calls are routed through the service centre to be passed back to the local branch – slowly, if at all. On paper this looks very efficient, but it is not effective because it alienates the customers. One UK bank has recently lost over a million customers through such insensitive pursuit of the bottom line. The customers did not go to another bank because they thought they would get anything significantly better – they were simply alienated by the increasingly bad service of their original bank. While cost-cutting can show up on the bottom line quickly, the huge cost of such a high rate of customer 'churn' is not so obvious for the first year or two, nor, later, is the high cost of finding new customers or trying to claw back old ones. In the longer term this bank has suffered a major financial hit by following efficiency at the cost of effectiveness. It over-played its Operational Learning at the cost of its Strategic Learning.

Airlines seem to be following a similar customer-unfriendly route. While proclaiming ever greater customer service, they are locked into an industry formula which seeks mergers and, particu-larly, 'code-sharing' – reducing costs by sharing resources between different outfits. But not all services are the same, which is why customers choose between them in the first place. So unless code-sharers can achieve the remarkable organizational feat of provid-ing precisely the same 'hard' and 'soft' benefits in their new alliance branding, they will antagonize previously loyal customers who find themselves flying on an airline they do not like with a service they do not appreciate. Differentiation for the long term is giving way to commoditization in the short term, at the expense of long-term shareholder value. Frank Vogl, writing in the *Financial Times*[13] gives a good illustration:

I had booked my flight from Brussels to Boston on Delta Airlines and my ticket said Delta as well. But as I walked down the boarding ramp I knew something was wrong: the stew-ardesses were not wearing Delta uniform. The logo everywhere was that of Sabena, the Belgian airline that is in an alliance with Delta, Austrian Airlines and Swissair.

It was an old European Airbus, not a spanking new Boeing 777 of the kind United Airlines used to fly me to Europe. The legroom in Business Class (my round ticket to Europe cost me more than US$ 3,000) was so sparse that it was a pleasure to fly onwards to my final destination from Boston in the comfort of USAir economy class. The steak that was served seemed as old as the aircraft. There were none of the individual video sets that I might have enjoyed in British Airways Business Class, or the sleeper seats provided by Continental.

Here we have a classic example of a knowledgeable, experienced traveller, willing to pay a premium price, finding that the emotional contract he had with Delta has been reneged on, and knowing to his acute frustration that there is not much that can be done about it at the time. Whether or not the legal contract was broken by supplying something which was not as specified is as yet untested, but the emotional contract certainly was, which releases the discerning buyer to shop around. It is particularly ironic that, as airlines increasingly proclaim their 'global coverage', they seem willing to trade their carefully nurtured individual characters for a morass of sub-optimal services. The economic argument is that this is the only real way to increase their global market share while reducing costs, apparently without asking the fundamental question as to whether increased market share is the best, long-term way of ensuring customer satisfaction and, therefore, sustained shareholder value. One particular issue that is not addressed publicly is whether it can be guaranteed that all airlines participating in a code-sharing alliance subscribe to the regulatory, safety and service standards of the highest quality member. In a commoditized service industry this would seem to be essential.

Frank Vogl ends his article by saying:

> To place shareholder interests above all other interests is a short-term strategy which can only end badly. Delta, by tricking me into a Sabena flight, is no longer my airline of preference and I have more choices today than ever. If a partner of a leading world airline crashes, the damage to the latter's reputation will be enormous – and the costs to it very high. The strategists of new global alliances, in all business sectors, should start taking account of such considerations.

Customers will begin to fight back against such short-term approaches and when they do directors and senior managers will be under very different pressures when attempting to increase shareholder value, because the new types of shareholder activists and the increasingly vocal pensioners or 'new owners' will ask much more discriminating questions of their policies, strategies and tactics. The rapid growth of the 'X Company sucks' websites to give anti-corporate information, especially tales of bad services or products will have a salutary effect on many executives. Increasingly, if they are found to be boosting the bottom line to ensure their bonuses to the detriment of their brand in the long term then they are in deep trouble. As brands are valued on the balance sheet, shareholders ask more penetrating questions about the consequences of short-term decisions.

This leads me to my second sign of hope. Current directors and managers cannot hold on to their jobs or their convergent thinking for ever. Two contradictory pressures are at work here. On the one hand, new directors and managers can be selected, inducted, included, assessed as competent and be developed to ensure their organization's capabilities in appropriate ways. On the other hand there are signs of a growing awareness among boards of the need to strike a better balance between bringing in new blood and keeping the more experienced but often more expensive directors and managers. Directors and managers are relatively expensive, and in the rush to cut costs they are obvious and easy targets. Whether cutting director and management numbers drastically is wise is another matter altogether. Both they and experienced staff may be relatively expensive, but that reflects the investment made in them over the years by the organization. If they have worked in diverse and turbulent conditions from which they gained a range of experiences, behaviour and learning, they are still valuable. Younger staff may be cheaper, but are not necessarily cost-effective in difficult and changing times. Sacking everyone over fifty, as a number of financial services companies and the National Health Service seem keen to do, can look highly effective to the bean-counters but, again, effectiveness is sacrificed in pursuit of short-term efficiency with unpredictable, but usually negative, impact on medium- to long-term results.

A third sign of hope is the emergence of more 'self-managed' groups across organizations. As part of a bid to cut managerial costs these are given specified tasks and resources and then left alone to achieve their results in the best way they can decide. Such groups are not in themselves a solution to either the alienation of customers, or the erosion of an organization's experience base, but they show some imaginative thinking which allows for a dramatic shift in organizational power. This move towards trusting people more, and a recognition of the ability of groups to learn and develop both internally and in conjunction with other work groups, is a step towards creating true Organizational Capability. Self-managed groups are not yet common. As the evidence against thoughtless downsizing grows, and the real power delegated to such work groups is made manifest and better appreciated, they could also lead to an abreaction. The real power of information amplification or attenuation lost by managers will become manifest. There may well be a lessening in enthusiasm for self-managed work groups among directors and senior managers as they scrabble to regain their lost power, status and control.

The fourth sign of hope is the growing debate on the meaning of the Information Age/knowledge worker era. This has focused directoral thinking on the need for both knowledge creation and continuous improvement as central organizational activities. The consequences of this are only dimly understood by directors, managers and staff, but they contain some revolutionary possibilities. As Max Boisot's work (see p. 16) showed, the emerging line of argument goes as follows. Knowledge creation is increasingly seen as the realm of the generation of intellectual property, which is a key investment for the twenty-first-century organization. Investments should be shown on the balance sheet, so encouragement of the creation of intellectual property rights should be seen as a key directoral activity in strengthening the balance sheet of a business. The only resource capable of creating such intellectual property rights is the people of the organization, not the data embedded in computer chips, therefore people should be valued alongside the intellectual property of the organization on the balance sheet. Training and continuous improvement are essentially profit and loss account activities, but intellectual property asset creation is definitely a balance sheet item. Only when people's learning appears both on the balance sheet and profit and loss account will the Information Age organization have arrived.

Three Values for Future Organizations

Is it possible to create capable organizations which have sufficiently integrated thinking, systems and behaviours to balance continuously the effectiveness/efficiency dilemma? I believe it is, and that we should. I am encouraged by the rise in the capabilities of computer-powered information systems to help, but not to dominate, in this area. I am particularly interested in systems with 'intelligent agents' (programmes for asking intelligent questions) built into them. These aid learning by assessing data patterns, questioning stated assumptions, and then creating regular prompts to question continually the information being put into the system.

Such systems seem to be powerful developmental tools with which people can increase their organization's capabilities. Where they coincide with self-managed work groups, and when directors properly clarify their policy formulation and strategic thinking roles to allow managers and staff to get on with the day-to-day work, then both the shape and processes of twenty-first-century organizations begin to emerge.

These are built on three basic organizational governance values which are only now becoming explicit. In the future there will be greater internal and external

- Accountability
- Probity
- Transparency

These will be assessed and critically reviewed more frequently than before by the owners, and the directors and managers. But, because of the under-performance and under-conformance of many private and public boards, this critical review will also come externally from shareholder activists, institutional investors, regulators and legislators, and pressure groups. Additionally, real-time information will be more easily available in the formal organization to both staff, customers and other stakeholders, subject only to commercial confidentiality. Each group will be able to see its impact on the total system, and will be measured regularly on its effectiveness and efficiency, which will teach it to improve and innovate continuously. This will in turn create a more positive emotional climate, more energy, and thus greater capability, within the organization, and with customers, so reinforcing the virtuous circles of learning. In such an approach people really matter, which will also mean that the present power of the many departmental boundary managers and mechanistic message-passers will be short-circuited. We are seeing the growing democratization of organizations.

Restructuring

As self-management becomes more common, reliance on people's intelligence and improved information systems will see flatter, less hierarchical organizational forms. The classic organizational pyramid structure will begin to give way to matrices, centre/periphery models and double loops of learning, all of them more 'chaotic' than many existing directors and managers are willing to concede. Career progression will be more horizontal than vertical, which opens up a whole Pandora's box of people-management issues that have yet to be addressed fully. It may well mean that as we have fewer senior people in organizations, so employees at all levels will have to be trained to become mini-direction-givers for their part of the organization, to ensure the integration of the whole system.

The fundamentals of balancing task achievement with effective social process, and effectiveness with efficiency, pose the biggest challenge for twenty-first-century organizations. Yet that challenge is also as old as time.

There is little fundamentally new in human nature. Much can be learned from what is already known if we have the capacity and patience to look and ask. Many useful organizational ideas and practices can be derived through the study of, for example, the Bible, the Talmud, the Koran and Buddhist scriptures. Study of Sun Tzu's *The Art of War*, Niccolo Machiavelli's *The Prince* or Karl von Clausewitz's *Vom Kreige* pay rich rewards. Lewis Carroll's *Through the Looking-Glass* is a very helpful text for getting into the ambiguity-tolerating, dilemma-focused, 'chaotic' mindsets needed to handle today's uncertain world. In modern times Mary Parker Follet, F. W. Taylor, Alfred Sloan, Elton Mayo, Kurt Lewin, Peter Drucker, Carl Rogers, Reg Revans, Chris Argyris, Fritz Schumacher and Charles Handy have all had profound things to say on the effective organization of people. Despite all the modern rhetoric about, for example, 'learning organizations', one can make a strong argument that the necessary intellectual framework was already in place by 1947, and was working in the newly nationalized UK National Coal Board. That it has taken another fifty years of stereotyped, formulaic thinking before the situation became so bad that people had to reconsider seriously their approach to organizational design and processes is an indictment of us. In most organizations learning curves seem to be low and slow when applied to effectively organizing capability.

So, what can we learn from the past and present which will carry us into the future?

CHAPTER 3

From Pyramids through Figures-of-eight to Complexity

The human condition leads most people to seek in their organizations both alignment (pointing in the same direction to achieve tasks) and attunement (emotional commitment to the tasks in hand and the values which determine the manner in which they will be achieved). They seek co-operation towards an agreed end in a congenial way. The organizational challenge for directors and managers is to create appropriate structures and emotional climates to achieve this. A selected personal history of the evolution of thinking about organizational structures, social processes and capabilities follows, which attempts to synthesize the important elements of organizational theory and practice into five distinct structures, and to discuss the appropriate emotional climates for each.

In addition to the three fundamental building blocks of organizing (see p. 2), the framework and language of organizing must begin with what people recognize, albeit sometimes dimly – the existing understanding of the idea of Organizing Capability that has existed for centuries. This understanding consists of four key elements:

- The formal organization structure as officially espoused
- The tasks which achieve its purpose
- The social-emotional processes to energize, adapt and co-ordinate the whole

- The emotional climate which, in combination with the above, finally decides how effective and efficient the organization is seen to be by customers, consumers and staff

The formal organization is what appears on the organization chart. The informal organization is what happens in practice. Formal, structural, elements of organizing are the means by which organizational structure and processes are communicated. This is the 'espoused view', described in recruitment brochures and annual reports, which often leads to the belief of managers and staff that there is only one way of describing the structure of their organization.

The formal organization is, however, only one of the four elements of organizing capability, and often the least important. It is simply the rationalized structure, drawn on our organization charts, to which we pay undue attention. One can argue that with the exception of the very few necessary 'command and obey' chains, all other organization structures are to some extent informal and so 'virtual', in that they exist at any given moment only in the minds of individuals, or groups of individuals, who find it expedient to agree what 'the organization' is at any given time, and to make that work. To claim that there is only one organization, and that it conforms to the chart, makes the heroic assumption that the vast majority of the people within it agree, and are both fully aligned and attuned.

Organizational reality bears little similarity to the espowsed structure or assumed emotional climate. Why do directors and managers mess it up so often? I believe that much of the answer lies in the over-simplistic views they hold about what is the 'right' sort of organization, as if there were only one answer. There is no single right model – there are only ones that are appropriate for present and predicted circumstances.

THE DEVELOPMENT OF ORGANIZATIONS

Formal Organizations

One of the earliest of modern management writers was the
Victorian Mary Parker Follett. She wrote:

> The fair test of business administration, of industrial organi-
> zation, is whether you have a business with all its parts so
> co-ordinated, so moving together in their closely knit and
> adjusting activities, so linking, inter-locking, inter-relating, that
> they make a working unit, not a congeries of separate pieces.

When reviewing the following structural designs it is helpful to
ask which might give you a working unit, and which a 'congeries'.

1. THE CLASSIC PYRAMID AND MODERN BUREAUCRACY

Organizations are human systems for reducing risk and uncertainty. Many power holders, both individual and corporate, in the
major economies of the world still cling to two mutually reinforcing, and often debilitating, concepts – that of the organization as a
hierarchical pyramid and that of the organization as a carefully
constructed machine – when combined, the resulting structure
hopefully enables them to create certainty.

To many directors and managers this is the only true image of
an organization. By using it they reinforce the over-riding importance of the vertical relationships between people in the pyramid,
especially between authority levels and other sources of power,
while diminishing the horizontal relationships which enable work
to be done by the people who happen to be around to do it. Such
directors and managers combine 'command-and-obey' behaviour
from the top of the pyramid with a never-ending flow of work
from 'the machine', with little or no chance for getting feedback
or tapping individuals' learning. Some national cultures, for example the Latins and the Germanics, feel that this is correct and

adhere rigidly to formal structures despite changes in the external environment. Others, like the Anglo-Saxons and the East Asians, can tolerate, and use, much higher levels of ambiguity and flexibility in their organizations. They are constantly shaping and reshaping their Organizational Capability, often on a daily basis. But they are constrained by the rigid hierarchy of the pyramid and are strongly encouraged not to challenge the hierarchy. So over time they feel trapped by it. From their perspective there is little they can do to improve or change their, or the organization's, lot.

The pyramidal structure and its associated processes create an emotional climate that is ultimately demoralizing to the human condition. People can work happily in such an environment for a time, but sooner or later they become bored, or unable to be creative, and then either escape by leaving, or retreat into themselves and into increasingly regressive forms of behaviour in order to maintain their sanity in an increasingly rigid organization.

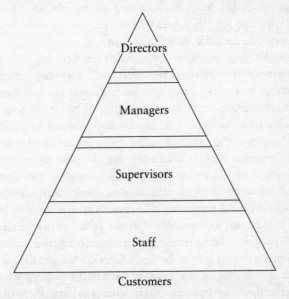

Figure 2 The classic pyramidal hierarchy

The power brokers sit at the top of the pyramid, usually deferring within themselves to one or two all-powerful individuals. Everyone in the organization knows their place in the hierarchy of power: jobs are formally defined and codified in great detail. Personal responsibilities and decisions are severely limited until you reach the very top. This focus on power and control makes many people feel abused and uncomfortable nowadays for two main reasons. First, as more people reach higher levels of formal education they expect to be at least consulted, if not to participate fully in the decision-making process, and this cuts across the essence of the pyramidal structure. Second, because pyramidal power and control are increasingly in opposition to some or all of the values of accountability, probity and transparency, which are the basis of all effective corporate governance and democracy. Accountability is increasingly seen as allowing delegation and authorization; but probity is often effectively screened out by over-tight job descriptions, which allow no chance for discretionary decision-making; and transparency runs directly against existing divide-and-rule power structures.

Pyramidal organizations are usually referred to nowadays in a derogatory manner as 'bureaucratic'. However, pyramidal bureaucracy has not always been seen as negative. The concept of structuring organizations hierarchically can be traced back to the founding of China some 5,000 years ago. Legend has it that the original pyramidal organization chart was drawn up to ensure that the then emperor was ensured sufficient choice in the provision of a fresh virgin for his bed each night. This pyramidal structure has endured through the Greek and Roman empires, through all military structures and the Roman Catholic Church into the modern day. It can be argued strongly that the first true bureaucrat was Philip II of Spain. His creation of the Spanish Empire was personally controlled and paper-driven. He ruled his peoples through long-extended lines of communication via the writing of reports and instructions, while complaining endlessly, usually in marginal notes, of the impossibility of his mammoth task. The British Empire took a slightly less centralized approach, but it should be remembered that at the height of Victorian power each night the

British Foreign Secretary wrote by hand instructions and advice for his ambassadors across the world. He was later aided by the head of the Foreign Office, who rejoiced in the title 'Chief Clerk'. The British Raj in India was run effectively through 200 district officers who wrote three sides of paper each week for transmission to Delhi and the Viceroy. One side was on the present situation, one gave ideas about future problems and events, and ways of coping with them, and the final listed any other items of note or interest which would keep Delhi sensitized to events. This worked very well for some 200 years, and was highly cost-effective.

In the twentieth century the pyramidal structure has been researched and described in detail by Max Weber, who saw it as one of the twentieth century's great contributions to the ascent of man. His seminal work *The Theory of Social and Economic Organization*,[14] published posthumously in 1924, argued that the depersonalizing effects of industrialization were inevitable. He thought that those in large organizations were required to give higher priority to the organization than to themselves. In contrast to Karl Marx's belief that industrialization trampled over the rights to the ownership of labour, which should be resisted, Weber was more pragmatic, and saw that the subjugation of individuals to organizations was a reality. A major problem of Weber's work is that it does not read like a treatise on pragmatism, but rather as justification for each bureaucrat being a carefully engineered cog in an increasingly efficient machine which brooks no deviation. Weber did not advocate bureaucracy – he merely described it, but his ideas, and F. W. Taylor's, were made manifest in the factories of Henry Ford in the US. Ford was obsessed by science and technology and not pro-people, leading to his famous plea: 'How come when I want a pair of hands, I get a human being as well?' Such concepts have remained in place throughout the twentieth century, and can be seen surviving strongly in the 1990s in the 're-engineering' fads whose mis-interpretation has led to so much organizational misery today. Bureaucracy continues. It is highly robust, and very useful to those in power, as it makes their power very clear, and difficult to dispute or negotiate.

Even in the late twentieth century, bureaucratic structures have a positive meaning in organizations where procedure and control are paramount. As I spend a lot of time at 39,000 feet travelling between the UK, Hong Kong and Australia, I am delighted that the Engineering Division of Cathay Pacific Airways keeps its excellent record through a clearly defined bureaucratic structure. It is reassuring to feel that people have done exactly the job specified, no more and no less, and that any questions were not dealt with on an ad hoc basis, but were referred to the rule book or upwards until they were answered fully, and then were recorded for future learning transfer.

The problem is that unless personal rewards for excellence are on offer then bureaucracies are rarely pleasant places in which to work. Where precision, excellence, strict adherence to rules and health and safety are essential such a structure is highly appropriate but work best in a stable, unchanging environment – internal and external. Once the environment becomes uncertain, complex and chaotic, then the pyramidal structural form begins to find it difficult to respond rapidly, usually tries to tighten its controls inappropriately, and begins to falter. Changing customer demands are seen as an increasing nuisance. Indeed, people at all levels often talk of the organization being better off, and much easier to administer, without customers: 'If only we could have a break from incessant customer demands we could get the place properly organized for once!' Ideas and pressures from the staff for changes are typically treated harshly and, if the external environment is forcing change on the organization, then those at the top often go into a long period of denial. Initially, they refuse to accept that the environment has changed, that things need to be done differently, that people other than themselves can learn to offer pertinent solutions for the organization, and consequently, that shifts of organizational power are occurring.

In its most advanced form in modern corporations the pyramidal structure has developed Chandler's idea of the 'divisionalized' structure – the breaking down of one large pyramid into many smaller pyramids linked within the larger one. This can be found in US corporations across the world. Each division can have a turnover equivalent to the gross national product of many a small country.

If the classic pyramidal model is insufficient in rapidly changing times, what other options exist?

2. THE INVERTED PYRAMID

A major change of view that seemed to double the vocabulary and portfolio of organizational structures was created by Jan Carlzon in the late 1970s with his book *Moments of Truth* (*The Inverted Pyramid* in the original Swedish).[15] Carlzon was CEO of Scandinavian Airlines System (SAS). The airline did not have a good reputation amongst its customers, and seemed unfocused in its markets and strategies. He and his team redirected it towards the business market and the specific needs of those customers – reliability and punctuality. These were aspects of service for which SAS was not well-known, but for which its business customers were willing to pay a premium. To achieve this he needed to refocus totally the company's purpose, vision and values, structures, processes and emotional climate. The top team set out to explain to the staff the reasons for overturning their comfortable but customer-unfriendly organization.

They consciously inverted the organizational pyramid. The customer was no longer to be seen as an annoying extra outside the 'real' organization who should be dealt with only when absolutely necessary. They argued that to survive as an airline in an increasingly competitive market they had to reframe their thinking so that the customer was at the top of the pyramid – the person whom they must serve consistently well if they were to have any guarantee of an income and a career.

It was everybody's job to ensure that the consumer's experience when they met any SAS customer-facing staff was positive, so that these accumulated experiences ensured the *perception* of SAS as an airline that delivered what it promised: punctuality, reliability, and good value for money, so that the customer would fly with them again. Until the inversion of the pyramid, customers and customer-facing employees had been treated as the lowest forms

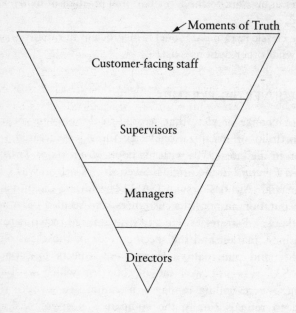

Figure 3 The inverted pyramid

of organizational life. Suddenly they became, both symbolically and in reality, the front-line face of the airline. The points where staff – especially telephone operators, check-in staff, and cabin crew – met the public were called 'moments of truth' by Carlzon. They had millions of these a day and many of them had been bad. A disgruntled customer usually tells at least six other people about a bad experience, so simple arithmetic explains the poor brand image of the old SAS. The directors and managers stressed that this had to be changed, by getting everyone to understand the importance of, and join in the process of, inverting the organizational pyramid – focusing on attitudes and behaviours which improve the customer's moments of truth, and make real the ideal of 'the customer as king'.

These key Organizational Capabilities evolved until it became obvious that the same thinking and values should be applied also to the 'internal customers' – the flows between the work groups.

This set in motion a 'whole system' transformation which continues today.

The acceptance by managers and directors of a major shift of power in the organization was of great importance in achieving success. I argue in *The Fish Rots from the Head*,[16] that at the day-to-day, operational-level managers are there to ensure that work gets done effectively and efficiently through the installation and maintenance of control and performance measurement systems. Managers should not get too involved in the detail – that is the responsibility of supervisors and staff. In operational terms directors are there only to oversee managers' performance, but not to intervene directly. Any intervention must come through their critical review and dialogue with the managers, even though their information management systems will show in real time what is happening at the moments of truth.

This was a major shift in power for SAS. It reinforced the power of customer-facing staff and the first-line managers to whom they reported. It emphasized not just the 'hard' tasks, for example getting 98 per cent of flights away on time every day, but also the impact of 'soft', interpersonal processes between individuals, work groups and customers. Where appropriate, staff were given small levels of discretion when dealing with a customer, so that more customer-friendly 'flexing' would be seen to go on, still within the 'rules' of SAS. A key psychological shift was to change the staff members' self-image from that of administrators of a static system to that of on-line problem-solvers in a dynamic system, balancing the customers' and organization's needs through the exercise of improved interpersonal skills. This has noticeably improved SAS's Organizational Capability, because it has an energising effect on staff, who have a more interesting and varied job to do, and on customers.

These concepts have been taken up successfully by organizations such as BA, Unipart and Rover. To change a culture in this way often takes around five to seven years – it is a very powerful process, but there is no quick and easy way of doing it. Inverting the organizational pyramid is a major commitment for a board of directors and senior executives. It means sharing much information and power which was previously exclusively theirs, and being willing to learn from the upward feedback generated by the staff. Neither is a comfortable experience for directors and managers, especially in the first months. It is an acid test of whether they really want to improve Organizational Capability, whether they stick with it, or abandon it. If the latter, then they have accepted the doubtful proposition that being no worse than their competitors is a sufficient vision to drive the organization forwards.

Achieving Inversion

Once the customer-facing staff are trained in mini-problem-solving mode then the three-way relationship between them, their supervisors and the customers, can be developed. Supervisors, or first-line managers, are often undervalued, but for an organization focusing on significantly improving the quality of its moments of truth they are vital as an immediate buffer between the customer and the line managers. Supervisors need problem-solving and interpersonal skills training to allow them to exercise their agreed levels of discretion, and to know when they need to call in their managers, who have higher levels of discretion.

To the customer this process should appear seamless if it is to achieve two key Organizational Capabilities. First, by accepting personal responsibility staff can usually be developed to resolve over ninety per cent of customer needs immediately. This helps ensure that the majority of customers continue their perception that your offering is good value for money, and so increases the probability that they will make a repeat purchase.

Second, the focus on customer needs should be intensified through the installation of a system of regular audits to examine very carefully the ten to twenty per cent of cases which are frequently proving problematic. This is done by keeping two Organizational Learning questions in mind:

• What needs to be done to reduce the deviances from our present offering?

- Are any of these deviances worth amplifying to see if a new product, service, or market segment can be evolved?

These two key approaches establish the ability to learn operationally and strategically amongst the front-line staff.

As customer-facing staff deal with more deviations from plans, middle and senior managers tend to find their roles evolving, as they become back-stops for the supervisors, and more importantly, spend more time in the design, implementation and maintainance of the organizational performance and control systems which enable the customer-facing staff to do their work effectively and efficiently.

Because many managers have learned to do their jobs only in a 'hands-on, task-only' way they may find the 'hands-off, system monitoring and improvement' role quite intimidating. This is not exclusive to inverted pyramid organizations, but it can be seen most clearly in them. Many do not enjoy the process of reflection and redesign, but do enjoy sorting out immediate crises, so much so that they will even create an occasional crisis if there is none present, to give themselves the satisfaction of resolving it.

Geert Hofstede, in *Culture and Organizations*[17], points out that this is a characteristic peculiar to UK, Irish, Danish and Swedish managers. The English word 'manager' derives from the Latin for the hand, and entered the English language in Shakespearean times via the Italian *mannegiare*, concerning the breaking of horses. It is hardly surprising culturally that many managers tend, wrongly, to take a hands-on approach. However in the eighteenth century the word 'management' also took an additional meaning from the French *menager*, which concerns the domestic economy of a kitchen. The latter is very much an emotionally nurturing, rather than a macho, value. It is the combination of macho and nurturing within any manager which the inverted pyramid organization faces head on. The managers need more retraining to enable them to adapt to their new roles than do the customer-facing staff and the supervisors.

Even more affected in terms of power and role shifts are the directors, who will have less to do with the day-to-day operations. They must, of course, ensure organizational conformance with policies, strategies, values and plans by reviewing operational performance on a regular and rigorous basis. Their main organizational roles are in the areas of policy formulation and strategic thinking (shown in the *learning board* model) (see p. 63). They must create the direction, alignment and attunement which will lead to Organizational Capability. Sadly, most of the directors that I meet are not trained in this way, if at all, so they continue to behave as managers or professionals, rather than directors, and revert to jobs below the level for which they are now paid. This causes a knock-on effect throughout the organization, and can lead to serious learning blockages. This is the route to organizational incapacity, and must be resisted – it is the classic case of the fish rotting from the head.

3. THE ARROWHEAD ORGANIZATION

The arrowhead organization takes the inverted pyramid organization a stage further. Two pressures are now forcing change on all our organizations. First is the apparent implosion of management. A combination of the high cost of managers, the transfer of power towards front-line staff, and the diminishing need for old-style managerial work, questions their old existence. Their systems-design, implementation, monitoring and maintenance roles will however grow, and more checking of the effectiveness of the integration of working systems – the organization's continuing capability – will be needed, together with more time coaching the front-line staff and the self-managed work groups, but fewer managers will be needed to handle this.

Second is the rapid expansion of the use of Information Management (IM) systems. The manager's role in amplifying or attenuating messages, up and down the formal structure, is drastically reduced when directors can also use the IM system and its 'intelligent agents' to give them a 'window' in real time to interrogate at many levels any part of the organization. They can see precisely what is occurring without having to go through the

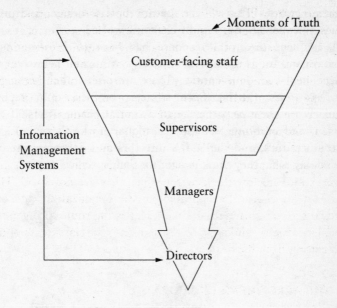

Figure 4 The arrowhead organization

formal managerial system. This may not always be wise, but it is becoming a noticeable habit among many directors.

Significantly, the 'arrowhead' organization shows a major behavioural shift in terms of organizational design. It accepts the necessity of multiple interactions with both the external world and the internal world of daily operations. The importance of identifying, developing and sustaining these interdependent relationships will be crucial as we move into the twenty-first century. The focus on sustaining the interactive system through the conscious introduction of learning systems – feedback loops – makes the arrowhead organization superior to the simple inverted pyramid.

4. CENTRE/PERIPHERY ORGANIZATIONS

One of the positive consequences of thoughtful business re-engineering has been to force organizations to completely rethink their structures. What will be the appropriate design, and processes, to cope with our rapidly changing world?

A frequent directoral response has been to break monolithic organizations up into units which can sustain themselves as independent economic entities. These are often called 'strategic business units' (SBUs). Such strategic business units report regularly on their performance to a central headquarters. If all is well, and everyone is happy, headquarters keeps out of the SBU's activities, and the SBU's directors and managers get on with doing what they think is right for their specified market.

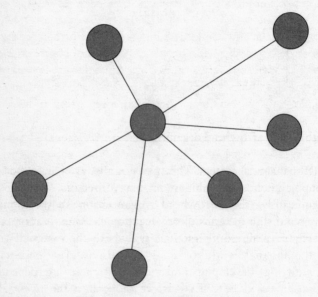

Figure 5 Centre/periphery organization

If an SBU under-performs, then it is supposedly easy to isolate it from the rest of the organization and either cure it, or get rid of it, without a massive effect on the performance of the others. Provided there is a reasonable distribution of central resources this works well. If not, then the organizational politics, as SBU 'barons' fight each other to influence 'the king' to channel resources their way, can become vicious.

The centre/periphery structure is perceived to have two distinct advantages. First, it focuses the mind of the SBU directors and managers on their own survival and growth. It helps to avoid one of the great organizational lies: 'I'm from head office, I'm here to help you.' Second, it drastically reduces the size and cost of the corporate head office, and so reduces the total corporate overheads. If SBUs sink or swim by their own devices, then the operational functions of HQ often shrink to just those of finance, strategy and people. HQs become more like wholly-owned merchant banks, deciding on distribution of resources, and how developments are funded on the basis of risk/reward calculations, in order to increase shareholder value. Wise corporate head offices know that they will need just a handful of policy formulators, strategic thinkers and people developers to ensure continuing performance across the group. Their function is to concentrate on long-term thinking and to develop suitable and implementable strategies, especially in finance and human resources, to back the business plans.

Within any SBU the usual range of organizational structures and processes can be selected, i.e. one SBU could be using an inverted pyramid, another a classic pyramid, while yet another could experiment with complex, adaptive structures. The suitability of the design depends on the rate of change in the external environment, the quality of the people in the organization, and the availability of resources to deliver the product or service.

5. MATRICES

Everyone in the organization can keep the working model of the first four examples in their head, as most people can visualize and think easily in two dimensions. But as organizations become more divisionalized, more international, and more prone to co-opetition (having both to compete and sometimes co-operate simultaneously with another organization),[18] the organizational model needs to reflect this increased complexity. Many people find it hard to visualize and think in three dimensions, let alone four, and so problems start in even understanding the basic structure and processes of 'matrix' organizations. Using matrix structures without very careful training in, and supervision of, the staff's understanding of them risks rapidly creating incapable organizations. Matrices have become fashionable, but many people cannot comprehend the deliberate and necessary tensions built into them. Such structures immediately challenge the old rubric that 'no one can answer to two bosses' by providing two bosses. One is usually the head of the professional discipline to which employees owe allegiance, while the other is often the head of the project group, or geographical region, within which they work.

For people accustomed to a pyramidal organization the idea that you can have two bosses is both difficult, and threatening, to grasp. The concept that the organization operates, simultaneously on two axes is challenging, and often leads to initial rejection. The two axes are usually designed around products and geographical regions:

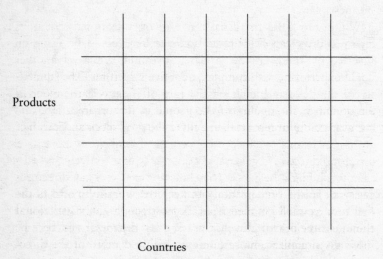

Figure 6 Product/geographic matrix organization

Alternatively, a projects and people development matrix can be used:

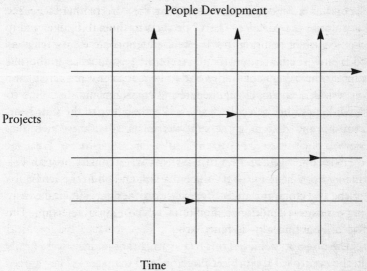

Figure 7 **Project/people matrix organization**

The more complex the matrix, particularly if an extra dimension is added by including time, the less likely it is that anyone in the organization is going to understand it. The process of creating global, multifunctional, manufacturing, project and product groupings begins to be seen by perplexed employees more as a directoral 'buzzword generator' than a way of effectively and efficiently running a business. The choice of axes is a key directoral decision. It is a fundamental because it dramatically affects the mindsets, reward systems, appraisal systems and the emotional climate of the organization for years, often decades, to come.

Matrix organizations can only be highly effective if the directors and senior managers really understand their structures, are committed to them, and act appropriately to demonstrate that they are managing a deliberately designed dilemma – the tension of, for example, the development of people, consciously pitched against the delivery of quality projects.

The best matrix structure that I have seen was designed for a defence electronics company. It took time to convince its staff that there was a fundamental dilemma at the core of their business: how could they deliver massive projects to time, to budget and to quality, while ensuring that their excellent people were developed to create even better science and technology, and were not burned out? Both of these conditions had to be met to ensure survival and growth in a rapidly changing external environment.

Making public the core business dilemma helped the staff enormously, and designing the organization so that these two axes were explicit was the key to the implementation process. Ensuring that the appraisal and reward systems were consistent with balancing both elements of the dilemma was crucial to the credibility of the directors and their organizational design, and in developing a positive emotional climate in which employees wanted to succeed continuously in both axes.

The directors achieved this by ensuring that budgets were firmly in the control of the project directors and managers. They agreed the 'hard' quantitative measures of time and money budgets, targets and project milestones. The 'soft', people development, qualitative measures, were treated equally rigorously. They created a personal, six-monthly appraisal system, and it was considered a sackable offence if managers did not complete their appraisals within a week of the half-yearly period end. The tough discipline of the appraisal system reflected equally the importance of both the task and the social-process sides of the organization.

Within a couple of weeks of the end of the six-monthly appraisals they effectively had a 'hiring fair'. All members of staff were put on an internal labour market, and the project managers had to bid to the directors to get them back. If they were achieving their 'hard' targets and were seen to also be using and developing their staff well, they got them back. If they were under-performing on the 'hard' side, then an immediate enquiry was held to ascertain how better to resource that project while maintaining the development of its staff (it was usually found that most under-performance was down to non-communication and interpersonal skills issues). If project managers were achieving 'hard' targets, but abusing their staff, then they were in trouble for not respecting the core organizational dilemma. They then either had to pay an internal premium to get their staff back, thereby upsetting their budget and increasing staff retraining time or, in very bad cases, their staff were withdrawn for rehabilitation and they had to go to expensive, outside contractors to deliver their project. This then caused them to under-perform on their 'hard' side because of their under-performance on the 'soft' side. The abused staff were transferred to better managed projects and/or retrained.

To tidy-minded administrators and bottom-line fixated directors and managers this sounds mad. After all, when the chips are down you just have to deliver the project, product or service, don't you? Not in the modern world. You have to deliver on both sides, particularly if you wish to keep the experienced staff who can help you retain your good customers, and so ensure your continuing profitability and growth. The example above has worked well for nearly ten years. They see their context as unique, and have a pride in being so different from other companies. I believe that their core dilemma is very common, but the difference lies in their recognition of that dilemma, and their use of the energies created by it. The designed tension in the organization, when used positively, gives huge energy to perform on both the 'hard' and 'soft' sides of their Organizational Capability.

Many oil companies, engineering companies, professional practices and global manufacturers have developed forms of matrices over the last two decades. Difficulties persist as people struggle to understand how and why they report to two bosses, one on each axis of the organization, but the matrix form has become well-established. Some companies have found that even matrices can grow fat and are beginning to slim down. One of the most successful – ABB, the Swedish–Swiss engineering and transportation multinational – was about to do so as this book went to press.

Of the five formal structures already shown, one can see that choices need to be made as to which is appropriate for all, or part, of your organization. Which will align and attune your people behind you, allowing directors to show the way ahead and give leadership?

And what of future organizational forms? Three distinct intellectual approaches are rapidly eroding the old certainties. There is nothing so practical as a good theory. All three, described below, add distinct benefits to our understanding of Organizational Capabilities. Note that all three are more process-driven, and emotionally more open and fuzzy, than what has gone before.

6. FEDERALISM – THE FUTURE OR A DEAD END?

Complementary to the idea of organizational matrices is the developing notion of 'federations'. This is also becoming highly fashionable amongst some consultants and academics, so much so that participants on certain MBA programmes have revolted against having to study too many 'federal' case-studies, especially the ABB Corporation. However, the thinking behind organizational federations is worth considering as a serious option in our turbulent times.

The essence of the idea is to expand and develop thoughtful, learning-based, co-operation between work groups, particularly those below the SBU level, i.e. too small to be economically viable on their own. These mini work groups (deliberately designed to be sub-optimal in size) have to agree to combine contractually with each other, either within an organization or between parts of organizations, to be of a sufficient size to be eligible to bid for work. They must then contract internally to bid for, and work on, projects. As many organizations are becoming a loose association of matrices held together by a small HQ, this process of agreement-building from the moment of deciding to bid is of great importance. The design assumes an internal contracting mechanism between the mini work groups. The process is essentially democratic, and involves voting on joint inputs, performance and assessment criteria, and the subsequent division of outputs from such co-operation. It forces open debate on the 'hard' and 'soft' aspects of organizing before the formal process of bidding for a contract in the external world starts. A federal organization putting together a tender for, say, a major power generation plant in East Asia would spend more time negotiating the internal contracts first than in more normal organizations, but would expect to generate better Organizational Capabilities and much better effectiveness and efficiency figures during the contract, and so better profitability figures at the end.

Again, many old-style project managers will write this off as a stupid allocation of resources, when the important issue for them is to win the project in any way that it takes. They argue that then will be the time to sort out in detail who gets what. But the companies using such processes are winning substantial, sometimes massive, international contracts in major industries like heavy engineering, rail transportation, electricity generation and information management. And they are delivering on time, to budget and to quality. What's the difference that adds the difference? I believe that it is the federal mindset and its associated processes.

A key aspect seems to be the initial formal negotiating process. In its purest form this involves the work groups voting for the terms on which they will participate in a project bid, and retaining this voting mechanism as circumstances change during, and at the end of, a project. This represents a significant change in the power relationships, and the emotional climate, of an organization, which releases high levels of energy, resourcefulness, resilience, and, especially, commitment.

Taken to its logical conclusion this structure could truly redefine the meanings of organizational ownership, participation, and industrial democracy in the twenty-first century, by allowing those directly involved in a project to control more of its inputs and outputs, rather than having them agreed in abstract at board level, and then being imposed without being emotionally contracted. It remains to be seen whether it will be a significant driver for organizations in the early years of the twenty-first century, or just an intriguing cul-de-sac. My bet is on the former.

7. THE LEARNING ORGANIZATION'S 'FIGURE-OF-EIGHT'

This has become an aspiration for many organizations. I wrote *The Learning Organization*[19] in 1986, to describe the idea of linking the internal, day-to-day, Operational Learning cycle of any organization with its external (policy) learning cycle, related to the changing worlds of customers, suppliers, pressure groups and politicians. Both cycles are systematically connected at the centre of a figure-of-eight by a 'business brain', which is the central processes of strategic thinking for the whole. The business brain is both a forum for organizational debate and dialogue for all levels of staff, and the place where the board of directors will ultimately take decisions on the organization's direction and leadership, while simultaneously keeping a watching brief on its operational performance and its legal and social responsibilities. This figure-of-eight model does not assume that only directors can learn, but that the whole organization is a complex, continuously learning and adapting organism.

A key assumption of the Learning Organization is that all people in an organization have both a right, and a duty, to learn consciously and continuously from their work. This necessitates an emotional climate, generated initially by the direction-givers and then sustained by them, which encourages open, transparent learning processes. These ensure the rapid admission of individual or group mistakes, an acceptance of responsibility to correct the problems, reflection on how to avoid them in future, and a commitment to implement appropriate solutions and to learn from them.

Such learning should occur at all levels of an organization all the time. It is the work group's responsibility to deal with the day-to-day operational level learning at the lowest level possible, and to codify this as part of the organization's collective memory. It is the managers' responsibility to seek the patterns in such continuous learning and to make sense of these patterns in relation to their organization's evolving strategy. The debate between the managers' views of the externally and internally orientated learning of their staff and these of the direction-givers are crucial to the ability of the total organization to learn.

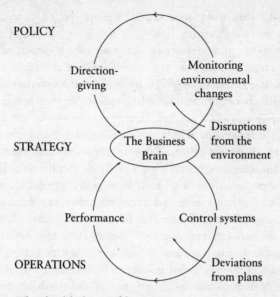

Figure 8 The double loop of learning, part i

Figure 8 The double loop of learning, part ii

To make this work it is crucial for the board to accept its pivotal role as a 'learning board'. It needs to balance and value both the external and internal learning which occur naturally from its employees' work, and to ensure that there are systems for capturing and debating this. In crude terms external learning directly affects organizational effectiveness (what is perceived by the customers), while internal learning directly affects organizational efficiency (the staff's deployment of its scarce resources to achieve that perception). Bringing these two together at the level of the business brain allows not only continuing dialogue across the organization but, most importantly, critical review and subsequent well-informed, and committed, decision-making.

There are many mechanisms for achieving this: from US General Electric's 'town meetings', where large numbers of staff meet together to listen to, and debate, key issues, thereby allowing the executives to take more informed decisions; to the real-time feedback of action learning groups facing and resolving a specific problem; regular feedback mechanisms from customers, suppliers, shareholders, other stakeholders and local communities; company websites; intranets; awaydays; workshops; encouraging 'whistle-blowers' etc. The necessary organizational technology is in existence. The big question is usually whether the directors have the will and the emotional intelligence to do it. As they have often created, consciously or unconsciously, the emotional climate that currently blocks organizational learning, their reluctance to face the issue is understandable but not forgiveable. Often it is only when an unavoidable crisis looms, which proves both urgent and irresolvable by their normal methods, that the organizational learning systems are opened up. At this point organizational energies, commitment and capabilities are often low – then, only their own people's rate of learning is capable of saving them. Henry Mintzberg, in his new book *The Strategy Safari*,[20] says that the idea of the learning organization is one of the few innovations in management thinking which is likely to rise above being just a fad. He thinks that it is here to stay.

8. COMPLEX ADAPTIVE SYSTEMS

'Complexity Theory' is currently a hot topic in organizational circles. It is also totally disorientating for 'Newtonian' managers, who believe in the certainties of a mechanical universe and the indivisible power of command-and-obey systems. Complexity theory is derived from quantum mechanics, and says that the universe is not, and never was, mechanical. Newton used the metaphor of clockwork, 'celestial clockwork,' to be precise, because it represented the most advanced thinking of his era, but time has moved on, and a better model is now needed to describe the turbulence of the world and cosmos.

Because complexity theory originates from the transfer of ideas that are not yet fully developed, from the scientific community into the organizational world, we need to be very careful. It is all too possible to be carried away by the excitement of the idea and the abuse of vocabulary which comes with it – as the glorious spoof by Alan Sokal and Jean Bricmont in their book *Fashionable Nonsense*[21] shows. The authors are two physicists who launched a scathing attack on 'post-modernism', 'deconstruction' and other modern mental vices. They submitted a paper full of pseudo-scientific jargon and fashionable artistic references to a refereed journal, and after it was accepted they excoriated writers, particularly French modernists, for their pretentious abuse of scientific language. They also frequently questioned the privileged status of science by over-stressing the importance of the context in which research is conducted, and in over-stressing the examination of the preconceptions of the enquirer until they were reduced to absurdity. Paradoxically, the sciences are trying to re-establish their credibility by stressing the rigour of their work, as distinct from the arts, at a time when research throws up more uncertainty and ambiguity than ever. At present the scientific community is not completely agreed that there is a science of complexity, but there is growing evidence in favour of it needing to be taken seriously.

As Bob Monks says in *The Emperor's Nightingale*,[22] many scientists in such diverse fields as physics, biochemistry and mathematics are excited by the apparently 'unified approach', or convergence, emerging from the study of complexity. Sometimes, laws discovered in one scientific discipline appear strongly to be applicable in all the others. Complexity theory seems multi-disciplinary, and is therefore beginning to be applied to the structure and processes of human organizations, particularly at such establishments as the Santa Fe Institute.

Complexity theorists' favourite concepts, taken from the fields of mathematics and computer science, focus on the central idea that 'things are not what they seem'. This makes sense to me in organizational terms. They study things which seem to be immutable – rational laws which then unexpectedly turn out to contain random elements. Simultaneously, apparently random phenomena can conceal hidden order. The fundamental question is whether *coherence under change* is the central enigma of such systems: what is constant and what changes, and how? Thus the object of their study is not merely the complex system but the complex *adaptive* system (CAS).

David Lane, of the Santa Fe Institute, a leading theorist, has listed in *The Emperor's Nightingale* four 'aphorisms', paradoxical presuppositions, about complex adaptive systems which seem to apply equally to organizations:

1. *Chance as cause.* CAS yield aggregate patterns that cannot be determined in advance – you cannot predict what is going to happen, no matter how familiar the inputs. These patterns are constructed from random choices, or chance, but this does not mean that just anything can happen, since constraints operate on the choices. So in a complex adaptive system chance, more than any immutable law, causes the outcome.

If that does not unnerve determinist directors and managers, then the next aphorism will.

2. *Winning as losing* (or, winning is not necessarily winning). In games theory this is made manifest as the 'Evolutionary Prisoner's Dilemma'. Evolution happens, sooner or later, usu-

ally later, when an ecology, or organization, is replaced because it fails to respond to a new challenge – organizations that die because they can not keep up with the rate of change in their environment. What is proposed in the 'Prisoner's Dilemma' is a model of a 'co-evolutionary' world of many agents in which 'an agent . . . that defines its success by "winning" against a currently dominant rival may find itself a "victim of its own success". Playing the new game well by the old rules does not guarantee success in the new game. Douglas Robertson and Michael Grant of the University of Colorado at Boulder find that 'because of the chaotic instabilities introduced by feed-back, natural selection will commonly cause fitness to *decrease*, in sharp contrast to the conventional view that selection only increases fitness'. This is where the new organizational thinking of the inelegantly named 'co-opetition' comes into play.

3. *Organization as structure and process*. Lane not only sees an organization as process as well as structure, but also challenges scientists to look at the inter-relationship of both 'to see how they mutually determine each other'.

4. *Rationality as limitation* (or, rationality is not necessarily intelligent). He says that one can succeed as an organizer without using rational planning, and quotes the undoubted success of Cosimo de' Medici, head of the Medici dynasty. He did not engage in rational planning but rather 'could feel the advantages his structural positioning in the network offered him, and he learned how to exploit the stream of opportunities that this position kept flowing in his direction'.

I realize that these four aphorisms will be a challenge to many directors' and managers' carefully nurtured rational and comfortable world view. However, it is worth persisting with them if they are to be prepared to cope with increasing uncertainty and complexity.

Bob Monks goes on to demonstrate how CAS can have a direct impact on the business world. He lists first the multiple corporate agents in the game:

- Owners (majority)
- Directors (management)
- Employees
- Customers
- Suppliers
- Lenders

All of these are internal to the corporation, and without them it could not exist. Each of these agents has interconnections with other agents throughout the corporation.

He then lists the multiple economic agents who also interconnect with the corporation:

- Owners (minority)
- Directors (non-management)
- Other corporations
- The general public
- Regulators
- The environment

It is the, often random, combination of such corporate and economic agents – chance meetings with buyers or politicians, managerial fads, or unexpected orders – which over time begin to determine which firm dominates a market. Over-elaborate, time-consuming, strategic planning has had its day, as Henry Mintzberg has argued eloquently in *The Rise and Fall of Strategic Planning*.[23] In a turbulent world strategic thinking is the key – strategic planning needs to be kept to the minimum. Brian Arthur concludes that 'the (corporate) economic activity is quantified by *individual* transactions that are too small to observe, and these small "random" events can accumulate and become magnified by positive feedback so as to determine the (positive) outcome'. That sounds to me like the organizations I know and try to develop.

Initially this may appear confusing, but I hope you will see that reliance on a mechanistic, organizational mindset alone is much more likely to create a learning system that is sickly and unadaptive rather than one that is healthy, complex and flexible.

Even if they are not convinced by the wonders of Complexity Theory, directors and managers still need to understand and be sensitized to the inner and outer complexities of the daily life, and the multiple, and often unpredictable, interactions of the people who comprise their organization.

Informal Organizations

Running less visibly, and very powerfully, inside any formal organization is the constantly changing informal organization – the way people rub along to get things done, or, occasionally, stop them happening. This is where the espoused direction, leadership and values are changed into behaviours. This day-to-day energy is generated by the individual, beyond the direct orders of the directors and managers. This is where the long-term energy and commitment is created which cause the organization to achieve, or miss, goals, and where agents interact, often randomly, to determine the emotional climate, long-term culture and future of the organization. It is the bane of deterministic managers' lives and it will not go away – ever.

Because the informal organization deals in emotions it also has its shadow side. It is the basis of the organization's 'rumour mill', and the system which endorses unconstructive behaviours and downright prejudice: 'old customs' as they are quaintly called in some industries. This is where the real corporate values are generated. They are based on a combination of highly personal values and beliefs, folk-histories and group aspirations, over which directors and managers have very little direct control, as they cannot order someone to only use one set of values to achieve an end. If they could, then all organizations would effectively become cults, where no one could challenge the central beliefs. Directors and managers can, however, influence people through specifying behaviours and rewards, so that the benefits of their desired objectives and values are made mutually manifest.

If around seventy-five to eighty per cent of a total organization understand the targets, and are roughly aligned and attuned to them, then the direction-givers are doing remarkably well. In these conditions an effective work group with a competent manager can make highly positive contributions to the customer's experience of the 'moments of truth'. The tasks are achieved, and because the emotional processes of the informal organization have been acknowledged and used constructively, staff are ready and willing to do it again.

Both the formal and informal aspects of Organizational Capability are measurable, and should be assessed regularly and rigorously by directors and managers.

CHAPTER 4

The E-motional Aspects of Organizing

THE DRIVING, AND BLOCKING, FORCES OF ORGANIZATIONAL CAPABILITY

Informal organizations are the day-to-day reality of working life. We all inhabit 'virtual' organizations, regardless of what the organization chart says. Organizational reality is what people and groups do, in interaction with each other, hour by hour. The formal and informal games people play,[24] within and between work groups, determine an organization's capability. The energy put into such games, and the aspirations people have for them, is determined by the personal beliefs, values and subsequent behaviours of each individual about the nature of the task in hand, and the appropriateness of the organization's structure and emotional climate in which they are asked to do it.

Hygiene Factors

One of the great frustrations of directors and managers is that the formal, visible, espoused structure and reward processes of any organization are known to have little long-term energizing effect on people. Frederick Herzberg carried out the classic studies which first signalled this.[25] He demonstrated, to many managers' concern, that the organizational elements controlled directly by directors and managers – such as financial rewards and physical conditions (hygiene factors) – are necessary, but not sufficient, to ensure the long-term motivation of staff. Indeed, even significant pay increases had only a very short-term motivational effect. People's spending rose quickly to accommodate the rise, thus triggering new pay demands. It is now generally accepted that over-concentration on financial rewards does not have a motivating effect.

In a leading UK bank loyalty bonuses and stock options were given, in addition to substantial salaries, to a few hundred senior managers and directors, if they signed a contract to stay with the bank for a guaranteed three years. Instead of driving the managers to new heights of performance the bonuses seem to have had the opposite effect. Most of them now feel that they are richer than they ever anticipated when they started their careers. They also realize that they will never make the very top of the organization. They have, if anything, eased back on their performance, and now begin their working day by checking the price of their stock, and spend time talking with each other about the best time they can capitalize their stock options, and so how soon they can retire. This is hardly the motivational investment for which the board voted.

Herzberg demonstrated that long-term performance came only through the motivators which were entirely controlled by the individual: recognition of achievement, personal satisfaction, the demanding nature of the work itself, relationships with their supervisors. Herzberg's slogan 'hygiene is not enough' still has real meaning for organizations trying to optimize the relationship between the 'hard', manager-controlled aspects and the 'soft', individually controlled aspects. Remarkably little has been done in most organizations to redesign jobs to accommodate it.

Why is it that these hygiene factors are so often ineffective, except in the very short term? It is a paradox of organizational life that, despite the lack of control felt by many staff, in reality they have some informal flexibility with which to pace their workflow, personal satisfaction and the recognition gained from it, without absolute regard to the formal organizational demands. They cope by balancing the seemingly rational economic demands of the organization – its targets, milestones and bottom lines –

with their own personal, or group, emotional trade-offs in the informal organization. If they have to meet targets then they will do it their way, and get their own satisfaction from it.

The Enigma code-breakers at Bletchley Park during the Second World War were often highly dedicated groups of very young, and very bright, people who worked ridiculously long hours in bad physical conditions for little extrinsic reward. One of their early triumphs was to break the Italian navy's code, and so get the battle plans for Matapan, leading to a notable victory for the Royal Navy. The code-breaking team were delighted with their achievement and the praises heaped on them, yet when Admiral Cunningham visited to congratulate them, the young women involved said later that they got nearly as much satisfaction in getting the admiral unwittingly to lean back onto a freshly white-washed wall in their quarters, 'leaving him with a whitened stern'. This was a task that they had set themselves.

Emotions

Informal organizations run mainly on emotions, which can be positive – concerning trust, co-operation, positive recognition and personal achievement – or negative – concerning anger, frustration and fear – but whichever they are, they are powerful drivers.

The classical root of the word 'emotion' is in driving forward – motion. Over time the word has tended to become too associated with 'an excited mental state, feeling, belief, or passion'. I like the definition given by Daniel Goleman in *Emotional Intelligence*.[26] 'I take *Emotion* to refer to a feeling and its distinctive thoughts, psychological and biological states, and the *range of propensities to act* [author's italics].' I use the term 'e-motion' in this text from now on when I wish to emphasise that I am talking about driving forces, rather than excited states.

Goleman lists the basic human emotions as:

Anger
Sadness
Fear

Enjoyment
Love
Surprise
Disgust
Shame

All of these can be experienced by an individual during a day's work, and are not necessarily over-reactions. We are not obliged to be constantly in an excited state to be emotionally aware – we are constantly affected by our emotions and initially most of us learn how to deal with them from our parents and environments. They help us to feel the benefits of the self-control of each emotion. However, in later life we can run into problems when we come up against people with different value systems and behaviours, especially if their systems involve the suppression or amplification of our emotions and the other party has more organizational power. Over-rational, or emotionally immature, directors and managers can try to suppress individuals' emotions but they will never be able to control them totally. It seems that a version of Newton's Third Law of Thermodynamics occurs – there will be an equal and opposite reaction. The energy will be transferred elsewhere, into opposition, obsession, or outside the organization into such foci as the family, or community organizations. E-motions are the social lubricants which keep people working on their tasks without over-heating or stopping.

Effective directors and managers understand that people are rewarded as much by recognition, thanks and personal development as by financial reward, if their energies are to be released to create capable organizations. Without the acceptance and use of emotions by directors and managers we risk slipping into seeing organizations as mindless machines. E-motions are manageable, but many directors and managers are not trained or developed in dealing with either individual or organizational emotions. What can be done to ensure the place of emotions in organizational life?

The Basic Values of Organizational Capability

One method is to ensure that the basic *values* of Organizational Capability are defined and built into the appraisal and reward systems of the organization. Daniel Goleman lists five key, emotionally-driven, values which I argue lead to effective Organizational Capability:

- Self-control
- Energy
- Persistence
- Optimism
- Co-operation with others

Combined, they reflect the concept of essentially self-managing individuals and groups, working willingly to meet the negotiated 'hard' targets. Surely this is what happens anyway? The difficulty is with the word 'willingly'. How can willingness be generated?

The converse of these values, according to Goleman, are the emotional obstacles to Organizational Capability:

- Irrational impulses
- Lassitude
- Grasshoppering
- Depression
- Social isolation

Sadly, these reflect the 'normal' view of many staff about their organization, and vice versa. This 'normal' emotional climate is often unwittingly created by apparently 'rational' directors and managers. Organizing so that the e-motional drivers of Organizational Capability are recognized and rewarded is a necessity for all effective managers and directors.

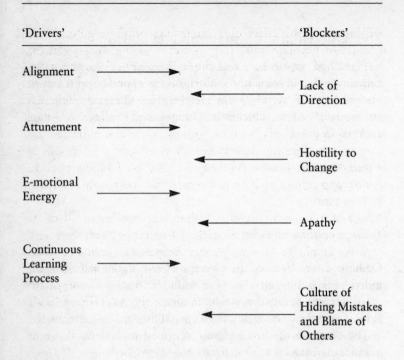

Figure 9 The main drivers and blockers of Organizational
Capability

APPRAISAL

One way to recognize and reward directors and managers for
their ability to nurture the drivers of Organization Capability is to
ensure that the appraisal system truly reflects the importance of
people management to achieving tasks. A July 1998 Gallup survey
in the US of over 100,000 employees in hundreds of different
units across twenty-four large companies, over twenty-five years,
came up with some interesting data. Despite all the published corporate rhetoric about mission and culture, the conclusion was
that what really matter are the relationships between managers
and their work groups. Units where employees were most satisfied
were usually by far the most successful.

Evidence of the effect of a dominant corporate culture was mixed. For example, only forty per cent of the workers in the average work group in a restaurant chain were happy, yet the company included some of the most successful and happiest work groups in the survey, while a financial services company with high average levels of satisfaction had some of the most dissatisfied workers in some of its work groups. Over-concentration on 'corporate culture' at the expense of work-group relationships is unproductive, but by contrast, focusing on building positive work-group cultures will build a constructive corporate culture in the long term.

As *The Economist*[27] reports Gallup will not reveal all of its clients, but they included Best Buy, Columbia Healthcare and Carlson. Employee satisfaction was measured in terms of those elements controlled by single managers: clear performance targets, availability of the right tools for the job, competent colleagues, and good supervision. Interestingly, ABB is mentioned as one of the few companies which publishes detailed comparative data on the 'hard' and 'soft' performance of its different production groups.

The survey reflects the perennial challenge for directors and managers: how do they get their people to give regularly and consistently of their best? Encouraging staff to use their emotional energies to learn through work is a clear answer, but creating superior performance through the promotion of superior learning is not a normal executive approach. Many executives claim to live in the 'real' business world, where the only effective values are hard, mindless work and blind obedience, usually coupled with mild levels of dishonesty and hypocrisy. If they do not accept that people can energize themselves then they risk creating a demotivated workforce and a culture of malicious obedience.

This 'blocking behaviour' occurs because many managers do not understand that energizing – motivating – people is a continuous process, rather than a one-off, command-and-obey order. Such managers assume that only the 'hard' side of organizing lies within their personal control, while all else is subsumed in a vast, anonymous whole called 'the organization'. This is patently untrue. You and I live daily in these managers' perceived 'unreal world'. Whose world is the more unreal?

An individual or group will assess relatively dispassionately how much effort they will put into a job to get what they consider to be an adequate level of satisfaction out of it. They are in full control here, not the manager or director. Bringing together the world of the formal organization with the personal, work-group world of the informal organization is the key to Organizational Capability. But how can this be done?

A Measurable Model Of E-motion

I have puzzled over this question throughout my working life, and have searched for the simplest model to explain the total formal/informal organization impact on an individual and work groups. I have always been attracted to a model published in 1968 by Porter and Lawler[28] which attempted to combine both the 'hard' and 'soft' sides into a motivational model. Over the years I have adapted it a lot, and hope that the authors will forgive me, but I have been learning too. The model is a powerful tool for explaining and measuring the relationships between financial rewards and non-financial rewards. It consists of a flow from left to right of inputs, effort and outputs, to give a measure of personal and organizational satisfaction.

ENERGIZING INPUTS

Tangible Rewards
The model starts on the 'hard' side with tangible rewards. Foremost amongst these are pay and conditions: the rewards package. There is no simple formula for this, but in any organization people will know the market rate for their job, the upper and lower quartiles, what benefits others get, and how they fit into this bigger picture. It is a subject of constant talk in any organization, particularly in the informal organization. Negotiating salary and conditions can become a major blockage

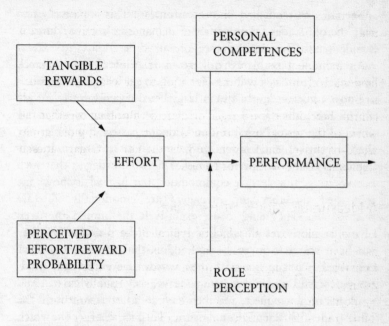

Figure 10 Inputs to the e-motional energy model

if they are seen as the only hygiene factors available to management and staff. Then, not just the rate of pay, but also the detail of holidays, annual hours, sick pay, medical care, pensions etc. can become the ground for prolonged negotiations. This absorbs a great deal of organizational time and energy which could otherwise be used more productively.

In regions where there is a surplus of labour, wages and benefits tend to be modest, but in areas of high demand for labour they climb rapidly. This has created two contemporary economic phenomena. First, the propensity of commoditized products and services to follow lowest labour costs around the world. In a couple of decades, previously 'developing' countries like Hong Kong and Singapore have moved from having an unskilled, cheap pool of labour to having an educated, expensive workforce, and now subcontract basic manually skilled work to countries like Indonesia, the Philippines and, now, southern Africa.

Second, the tendency for professionals and top executives to play the old trades union games of demanding 'the market rate' coupled with 'the maintenance of our differentials' to extract the maximum possible tangible rewards. 'Golden hellos', stock options and bonus payments for modest performance increases are now common, especially in large listed corporations. We are all the unhealthier for them. These are seen at their worst in the financial centres of New York and London, where companies pay their executives and traders very large sums for often loosely defined and assessed 'performance'. This would suggest that such people are genuinely rare commodities, but instead it shows me that their directors and managers are emotionally illiterate businessmen. They tend to use exclusively the limited approach of money-motivates-all which is typical of hard-siders. 'We pay you well so perform or be sacked,' is the message, but their behaviour is not in line with their words. If even an only modestly successful trader threatens to leave, they usually cave in and grant his or her request, and then have to adjust upwards all the other traders' differentials, unless they keep the deal secret, which many try to, thereby creating a culture of mistrust.

Pay never remains secret in an organization, and when the new deal is found out the emotional climate becomes poisonous. Implicit in such an approach is the idea that in these types of organization there is no time to learn and develop, which could explain their increasingly high rate of turbulence and failure. From chief executives to young traders, people are brought in and expected to perform from day one, with little effective induction, inclusion or competence building from their line manager. Corporate amnesia seems to be accepted as the norm while conscious and sustained learning is ignored. Such an approach is highly cost-ineffective.

Perceived Effort/Reward Probability
The informal side of energizing starts with a calculation, both rational and emotional, by the individual or work group, of the probability that a given amount of effort will bring a given reward. People ask themselves: Can I just coast along, or does this

task really require an exceptional push? Will the rewards, tangible and intangible, be worth my making any extra effort than usual? Such calculations are learned quickly in most jobs at any level of an organization. When individuals begin to make similar and agreed calculations a work group's emotional climate emerges. Over time the aggregation of many work groups' thinking creates the organization's culture, within the framework the directors have designed. At this point the benefits of the contractual idea of offering personal development to ensure 'employability' can have a marked effect, by helping to ensure that positive energy continues to flow from employees.

Effort

Tangible rewards and the effort/reward probability combine to give a level of effort which will lead on to a level of performance. The e-motional energy level is set here.

However, effort is modified by two other factors:

- Personal competences
- Role perception

Personal Competences

The combination of an individual's attitudes, knowledge and applied skills is partly inherited, but is mainly created by the organization's attitude to the investment in training, development and employability it is willing to make. Individuals' emotional contracts, in addition to their legal employment contracts, with their organization clearly reflect this, especially at the directoral level, where often no investment is made at all.

The importance of measuring individual competences is increasingly acknowledged in organizations throughout the world. Most companies take a modular approach, i.e. that any piece of work can be reduced to a number of individually measurable elements, each of which is assessed separately. When added together these are said to represent the overall competence for a job. This is doubtful, as such an approach fails to assess the whole – especially the real-time judgements which have to be made in any job to allow the resolution of the problem presented. Sadly, many organizations use this 'tick boxes' method because it appeals to tidy-minded administrators, but it does not encourage the action-learning culture needed for capable organizations.

This is not to attack the assessment of competences. Such measurements are necessary and, treated holistically and developed systematically, they can be very powerful in creating Organizational Capability. It was stated in the Gallup study (see p. 77) that one of the key elements for worker satisfaction and performance was the possession of the right tools for the job. This must include competence-building. It is particularly true in knowledge worker organizations where the workers are their own tools: such tools need regular nurturing, maintenance and development.

When systematic competence-building is blended with regular upward feedback, or, even better, 360 degree feedback (see p. 122), then you have a strong foundation stone on which to build Organizational Capability at both the individual and organizational level. Ultimately, the application of continuous learning, developed through frequent feedback about the consequences of the organization's measured competencies determines both effectiveness and efficiency.

Role Perception

Individuals and work groups also put more or less effort into their work depending on how they see their role in the organization. At the operational level staff can either be paid to work hard and accurately, or can be a bit more flexible, provided the supervisor always gets, say, the work done and his or her coffee on time each morning. I remember the chairman of an international company who seemed to have to do only two things to rub along. First, to carry out the 'ceremonial duties' around the company which other directors found irksome. Second, to ensure that there was always a twelve-pack of tonic water in the group chief executive's fridge each morning. On arrival in the morning, the chairman was sometimes seen leaving his chauffeur-driven limousine clutching the bottles. He was very clear in his role perception about his relation to a very powerful industrialist, and it was part of the organization's folklore that this was a key part of the chairman's role. Whether this was appropriate or not is another matter. Ensuring positive role perceptions is a job for each line manager, but the problem for many company chairmen is that they do not have a line manager.

Often work groups, consciously or unconsciously, benchmark not only their pay and conditions against other, tightly specified, work groups, inside or outside the organization, but also their perceived status in relation to society. It is well-known that certain work groups set the aspirations of a country's annual pay round. In the UK, Ford usually sets its pay levels first, and thereby creates the target. Civil services often benchmark against agreed private-sector levels. Role perception also comes into play here, depending on which pay quartile people find themselves in, and to which they aspire. Pay does not determine role perception, but it indicates an organization's values and priorities through who is rewarded well, and who is not.

At the strategic level similar processes are at work. Company directors increasingly argue that they should be assessed against their top quartile peers. To make this credible they will need to be more openly assessed on their four key roles of policy formulation/foresight; strategic thinking; management supervision; and accountability. At present most are not. Acquired role perception can conflict with directors' engrained behaviours: the need to take time to think and reflect before giving direction can sit uneasily with their long-learned managerial habits, developed when they coped with crises day-to-day, which ensured a hands-on, rather than a brain-on, approach. Directors' roles can be learned, but at the start of this learning process it is difficult for a director not to feel guilty about reading a serious newspaper at the start of the day and spending time reflecting on, and codifying, what the changing external environment means for the future of their organization – despite the fact that this is a key element of the directoral role.

Role perception can be the bane of line managers' lives. It is extremely difficult to control directly a work group's or individual's perception, simply because it is so personal. However, it can be influenced positively, so long as the manager remembers that the effects spill over from work life into family, social and recreational life. Role perception is part of the emotional anchor system of an individual that gives measuring to their life. A line manager's positive influence in this area needs to be subtle to ensure that it does not reinforce a negative stereotype of the organization or the individual.

Performance

The level of effort in an organization is modified by competences and role perceptions to give a level of measurable performance; and the consequences of such effort are modified in turn through personal learning. The organization has only limited sway over what occurs in terms of the energized outputs.

ENERGIZING OUTPUTS

The level of output (performance) is increasingly measured through the achievement of tasks and, in a few far-sighted organizations, through the quality of the behaviours and values which led to this achievement. In the energizing process two measures need to be kept in mind: both revolve around personal expectations of the outcomes, and both ask the basic question of whether employees received the rewards they expected.

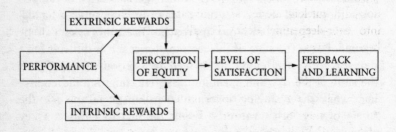

Figure 11 Outputs from the e-motional energy model

Extrinsic Rewards

'Extrinsic rewards' are outputs from performance, identical to the inputs of tangible rewards which are received as the basis of the employment contract. If they meet employees' expectations, at least half of their aspirations are realized, and then their focus switches to the more intangible aspects of the reward process. But if the expectation of tangible rewards is not met, then there will be trouble at some point. In societies with good labour laws any breach of the employment contract can be dealt with through the legal system. Sadly, many countries do not have tight labour laws, and so people resort to strikes, work-to-rule, and occasionally riots, when they feel the employment contract broken.

In a healthy organization, if managers recognize the difficulties inherent in changing the employment contract, they can use a blend of extrinsic and personally generated 'intrinsic' rewards to reset aspirations, and defuse the issue. In an unhealthy organization, especially one where managers feel that they are in absolute control, the staff can react negatively, and managers will not get the willing help they need. At worst, malicious obedience and obstructive behaviours can result in organizational under-performance, or even incapability. At the worst for the individual, failure to deliver the employment contract can result in human rights abuses as seen in the indenture systems found in South Asia and Africa. There, people deliver to contract, but are then deliberately faulted on some minor and debatable detail, are not paid but lent money at penal rates of interest, and so forced into ever-deepening debt. To all intents and purposes they become slaves.

Intrinsic Rewards

These reflect on the personal, emotional expectations of the satisfaction to be gained from doing the work. Was my work recognized? Was I thanked for my contribution? Did I enjoy performing at this level of effort? What did I learn? Could I have done it better, or could I have eased off without damaging the output? Was I able to do the work within my ethical values? Did

I provide for my family? Did I feel good in being able to satisfy that particular customer's needs? Do I have enough money to take a holiday? Am I maintaining or increasing my employability? These are the keys to gaining sustained working quality in an organization. They are often so personal that they will not be expressed to a line manager for fear of ridicule or non-comprehension, but their invisibility does nothing to reduce their power.

Perception of Equity

Both extrinsic and intrinsic rewards are checked against the individual's 'perception of equity' – their view of whether fairness operated during the work. Did all other things remain equal while I did the work? Was my effort/reward probability calculation justified? Am I being rewarded for what I was asked to do in the way I thought I would be on both the 'hard' and 'soft' aspects? Did the managers move the goalposts after I started the work? If so, am I still being treated fairly?

The time-span of the work is important, and must be considered seriously. If a job cycle is short, then the effect of the effort/ reward calculation will be rapid, and any amendments can be dealt with quickly by both parties. If they are not, then cries of 'I was robbed!' will be heard. Resentment can build, storing up medium- and long-term problems for both line managers and directors. If people are working on a medium- or long-term project, then much can change between the original personal and group effort/reward calculation and the 'hard' and 'soft' results. If the 'hard' expected results have not been well-recorded at the start, and the emotional side of the contract not been agreed alongside the targets and milestones, then, as the environment changes a perception of inequity may be created: 'They changed the goalposts halfway through the project, it's not fair.' This will sour the emotional climate and lead, in the long term, to organizational incapability. People will not keep responding with committment and energy unless they are systematically informed by the directors and managers of changes in the environment which will alter their perceptions of equity. The emotional and the legal side of the work contract will also need to be renegotiated to avoid people feeling that: 'They do not appreciate us and keep changing the rules. No one understands what is going on – so we will do as little as we can get away with.'

The effects of getting the perception of equity wrong can be measured and described through an Organizational Capability survey, but it should be remembered that a sincere 'sorry,' followed by an appropriate change of behaviour from directors and managers, can go a long way to rectify a soured emotional climate.

Level of Satisfaction

This happy state occurs when the 'hard' tasks demanded by the organization are fulfilled simultaneously with the 'soft', emotional demands. This convergence is crucial for full satisfaction. The euphoric state of full convergence is rare in organizational life, but it need not be if one understands, and behaves in line with, the e-motional processes. When it does occur dramatic improvements in organizational effectiveness and efficiency take place.

It is important to reiterate that directors and managers are totally responsible for the hard inputs: tangible reward, competences and working environment. Individuals translate these through their own value systems and behaviours into the 'soft' aspects: effort/reward probability calculation, role perception; performance and intrinsic reward. The directors and managers have to ensure there is sufficient, regular and rigorous feedback on both the 'hard' and the 'soft' sides to keep the emotional climate positive and so drive the organization forwards. They are ultimately responsible for ensuring the organization's capabilities, so that an emotional climate is generated where people can learn regularly and rigorously for the benefit of all.

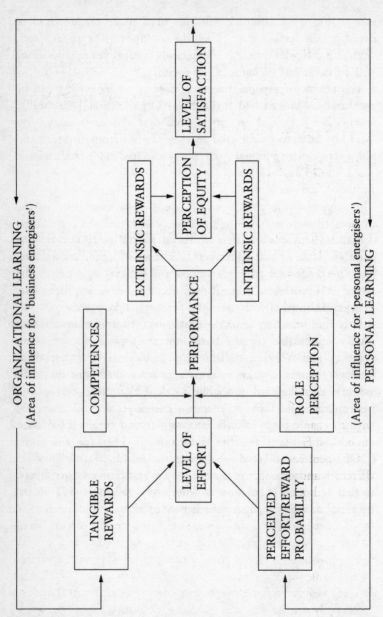

Figure 12 The e-motional energizing process

CHAPTER 5

Developing the Emotional Climate of the Organization

THE DIRECTORS' AND MANAGERS' ROLE IN CREATING AND DEVELOPING THE CULTURE OF ORGANIZATIONAL CAPABILITIES

How can directors and managers develop sustained energies and satisfaction both for themselves and their staff? This is the holy grail of Organizing Capabilities. The majority of staff must be roughly aligned and attuned to their tasks for an organization to exist at all, but crucially, they must also have sufficient e-motional energy and commitment to implement what is proposed. The source of such energy is generated, or not, by the top of the organization – that is precisely why my previous book is called *The Fish Rots from the Head*.

Of equal importance is whether the espoused values of the directors and managers are seen by the staff to be in synchronization with their behaviour. Do they truly 'talk the talk'? We are all used to reading company visions, mission statements and value statements which are not just useless, but a source of continuing irritation, even derision, throughout the company.

Reviewing such statements, it seems that every organization wants to be number one in the country or the world. Well who would wish to be number seven in, say, south-east London? Everybody wants to be 'excellent', or 'customer-driven' or 'working as a team'. I cannot think of an organization which would say otherwise publicly, yet the very frequency of such statements demeans and commoditizes them. I know of a few who argue that such phrases are a necessity, most do not. The managing director of a personal computer company says, off-the-record, that most of his customers are so ignorant of technology that 'they wouldn't care if it was driven by a rubber band so long as it was reliable'. Such honesty is rare. His business approach is 'We give you a quality box of tricks, you give us the money,' but he is only too well aware that any such public statement would be suicidal. He remembers vividly the effect that such outspokenness had on Gerald Ratner and his eponymous company when he made disparaging comments about the quality of his products, the shares crashed and he was ousted as Chairman. So out comes the well-worn rhetoric which neither staff nor customers believe.

And that's the rub. Unless an organization's purpose, vision and values are clear, and the words and behaviours synchronized, then all the time and energy expended on the production of such statements is wasted. Staff watch for this lack of directoral honesty like hawks, and transmit any mismatches with surprising speed through the informal organization's communication systems. 'Did "they" say that we had to have ten per cent headcount cuts? Well, did you know that the directors have taken on two more personal assistants which were not even in their budgets!' 'You remember all the investment in training that went into last year's product excellence programme? Well, did you hear that to meet year-end targets they let us ship sub-standard kit for four weeks just to get their bonuses? The kit will be returned of course, the customers will be furious, and we'll have to do them again, but the directors seem happy.' This goes on repeatedly in organizations around the world, and the directors' and managers' failure to see the connection between their words and actions often destroys the highly motivational 'perception of equity'. As this is the key to both ensuring satisfaction at work and to re-energizing people such an omission can have dangerous consequences.

The connection between directors' and managers' words and actions helps to dictate the emotional climate of the organization – for better or worse. Their actions clearly demonstrate who and what is really rewarded, who is punished, and just how far this is out of line with the statements by the chairman in the annual report. Over time the emotional climate of the organization becomes its 'culture' – the symbols, signs and values, attitudes, behaviours, skills, rewards and punishments which tie everyone in the organization to the 'webs of signification which we ourselves have spun'.[29] Each element of culture listed above is identifiable and measurable, but sadly this is rarely done on a systematic basis.

The Learning Board Approach

What can be done? Looking at the top right hand corner of the learning board model (see p. 63) we can start with policy formulation and foresight. These are focused on the long-term and external worlds of an organization. Policy sets the long-term context in which all other directoral and managerial decisions are taken. To do this effectively distinct values, attitudes and behaviours need to be developed by the direction-givers, and tested regularly with staff, suppliers and customers, to ensure that policy can be translated effectively into strategies.

It is essential that directors and managers give sufficient time for scanning and debating the changing external environment, so that sound foresight is possible. If the directors are sensitive to their organization's strengths and weaknesses – its Organizational Capabilities – then awareness of changing opportunities and threats in the external environment allows for better risk assessment. Direction-givers become faster, more informed and more sensitive about taking business decisions. The emotional climate of an organization becomes more positive if staff can see that their direction-givers are actually giving direction, rather than acting as over-paid managers, prone to intervening in operational crises.

PURPOSE, VISION AND VALUES

Within the policy formulation and foresight quadrant there are three major areas of decision where directors must exercise their role competently:

- **Purpose.** Why is the organization here? As we enter the twenty-first century it is necessary, but rarely sufficient, to say in the private sector 'to make a profit'. If you are not doing that, you die. Organizational purposes can be as simple as Microsoft's ensuring 'a personal computer on every desk and in every home' or Fife Health Board's 'to promote health gain in this region' to IBM's 'We shall increase the pace of change. Market-driven quality is our aim. It means listening and responding more sensitively to our customers. It means eliminating defects and errors, speeding up all our processes, measuring everything we do against a common standard, and involving employees in our aims.'

  For a closely-held company the purpose could be to develop and maintain the lifestyles of the owners. For a family business the purpose might be to ensure the continuation and improvement of the family wealth. For a parastatal company it might be to guarantee the supply of good quality water, or electricity, to the nation.

  Note that these core purposes do not need to be especially exciting in themselves. Purposes do not need to be dressed up in public relations-speak – they are too important, too profound, for that. Consider a health authority's purpose of improving health in its region. This is usually assumed to mean that within the existing provision – of general practitioners, hospitals ancillary services, and, especially, existing budgets – they should do their best. Yet effective health authorities spend time thinking about policy 'outside the (budgetary) box'. They benchmark the existing levels of health, and then think strategically about what other elements of the environment can also be used to help health gain, e.g. whether better sewerage, housing and policing could achieve the authority's purpose, even if it meant cutting back on its existing National Health Service spend. The very best health authorities will do deals with other public and private organizations to use optimally their total budgets to achieve their purpose. This is a lifelong task and, when done properly, will meet all sorts of opposition, especially from politicians and civil servants defending their own budget allocations.

I once worked with a governmental statistical department and, after much debate, we decided that the real purpose of the department was 'to illuminate the public debate on governmental policy'. Needless to say, this was not agreed by the ministers, who insisted on a much more anodyne statement. However, it became the unofficial, informal purpose of the department, and certainly energizes staff to this day.

• **Vision.** This needs to be more exciting than the simple statement of purpose. It is a picture of what the organization could be like in the long term. Unlike a mission statement, the vision should not be achievable in the short or medium term. Visions are meant to excite people and give them the e-motional energy for the long haul. In China there are classic paintings and drawings of the five-clawed, emperor dragon stretching out fully to try and capture the flaming pink pearl of knowledge. He never succeeds, but he is always trying. In the same way, good vision statements keep people stretching for much more than the achievement of 'hard' targets and budgets: they also give long-term emotional satisfaction to the organization, work groups and individuals. A large pharmaceutical company's vision is to become the world's leading 'green' pharmaceutical supplier. It has made some significant investments in this area, which feature as projects in its mission statement, but no one knows when or precisely how they will achieve their shared vision. It is a super-project in which everyone can learn to help take small steps along a road of unknown length. The vision is unplannable, but it excites people, so that they are keen to align and attune behind their direction-givers.

The idea of the deliberately unachievable vision which gives an organization 'stretch and leverage' in policy and strategy terms has been developed further by Gary Hamel and C. K. Prahalad in their book *Competing for the Future*.[30] At its simplest, vision can be understood through the traditional example of a visitor talking with a group of mediaeval stonemasons. When asked what they are doing, most masons answer that they are carving gargoyles, trimming lintels etc. But one says 'I am building a cathedral.' He is the one who understands the vision.

Without vision organizations just bumble along, unenergized, unresponsive to their changing environment, until eventually they cannot be differentiated from their competitors, can compete only on lowest price, become commoditized, and finally collapse.

- **Values.** Paradoxically, the production of a values statement is one of the easiest ways for directors to demotivate their organization. A proclamation by the directors of their considered values for the organization – usually unimaginatively based around a standardized list comprising excellence, integrity, quality, customer satisfaction, shareholder value and teamworking – is not taken seriously by the staff. It is only serious if each value is benchmarked, improvement programmes are put in place, and regular and rigorous assessments are made of individual and group behaviours to ensure that they are in line with the espoused values.

I know only a few values programmes like this. 'Values' has two distinct meaning in English: one concerns price, the other, emotional meaning. It is easy to confuse them, or to allow another person to think that you are only referring to one aspect of the meaning. For example, I was doing some work with a financial services company. The directors proclaimed their seven values, one of which was probity – they considered this a fundamental value for any such company, as, in their eyes, financial services are built on honesty and trust. After a struggle the directors agreed that we should benchmark each of their seven values by taking a sounding of the staff. They were astonished to find that the staff ranked them low on probity. The examples of a culture of organizational dishonesty were numerous: customers were regularly charged interest at too high a rate, or for a day longer than was necessary, or money was not credited to a customer's account until four days after it was received to avoid paying interest, or they were not informed if better accounts existed for them. None of these actions amounted to grand larceny in the directors' eyes, indeed they argued that they were protecting the shareholders' interests, but an anti-customer culture had grown up over a long period and had become systematic. Over time these tiny amounts added up to serious money. The customers were blissfully ignorant of both the problem and the possible solutions. Some of the staff kept asking: Is this honest? What value system are we really using here? Does increasing shareholder value mean that we must take these unsavoury actions? For that company the answer is 'yes'.

For the time being the directors have removed probity as one of their core values while they have a serious rethink on what, and how, they reward in this area; and how they deal with a demotivated staff, some of whom feel that they are led by people with decidedly low ethical values. This problem can be found in many other organizations, both private and public, and is particularly prevalent in the fee-based professions where a partner or consultant has great discretion as to what amount of time to charge to a client.

A key method of avoiding such an outcome is to involve staff in the creation of a values statement, and its implementation, from the beginning. This involves a two-part process. First, getting directors, managers and staff to generate independently six to ten values, both commonly held in the organization, and those which they wish were commonly held. These differences between directors, managers and staff can then be highlighted in joint sessions to test their validity against actual behaviours seen and rewarded in the organization. Directors and managers often find these sessions uncomfortable, but they can be helped to quickly focus on the core values, and especially on what is seen as good and bad behaviour in their organization. Even if they are then left with a list of negatives, this is useful data, as the process itself usually releases sufficient emotional energy in the staff for them to be willing to do something about changing the values. Value systems created in collaboration with the staff have levels of commitment undreamed of by most directors, unsurprisingly, as an agreed value and reward system gives meaning to people's working lives.

Second, once a set of positive values has been identified it can be turned into two or three specific and measurable behaviours. These behaviours can be designed so that they form fifty per cent of the appraisal system, which should ideally be linked to a 360 degree regular feedback process. The other fifty per cent of the appraisal comprises the measures of task achievement.

While it is common to measure task achievements against budgets, milestones, sales etc., it is less common to measure them against values. For example, if a firm aims to hold a value of probity, the measures might include being seen to account for all monies entrusted to it; being open in reply to questions from colleagues and bosses; and being fair to customers or suppliers when they raised queries or complaints.

Such an appraisal system can have a positive motivational effect on an organization because it rewards openly agreed 'good' values-based behaviours which help to achieve both 'hard' targets and the long-term vision. It can simultaneously punish or modify 'bad' behaviours and values through low scores. In this way, 'macho managers' who score high on task achievement will not get high rewards until they develop their social-emotional attitudes and skills in line with the organizational values. People who are too 'emotional' are also in the same position until they learn to balance better their emotional processes with their task skills. Collecting data regularly from both the task and social-process sides can target investment in training and development needs, and so greatly reduce the spend in these areas.

For those directors who find it difficult to accept that the convergence of their individual and group words and actions create an emotional climate in their organizations, I refer them to examples from UK public enquiries and coroner's courts. Here the public's right to know how a tragic personal or organizational failure happened is crucial to learning how to avoid future accidents. The railways, football stadia, shipping, airlines, pharmaceutical and chemical companies have all been held to account recently.

Chillingly, in the vast majority of cases, in the evidence, or the summing up, a sentence appears which says something like 'There was sufficient data inside the organization to avoid the accident. The major problem was that there were neither the systems, *nor the emotional climate* to move this data to where it could be used.'

This is epitomized in the Sheen Inquiry into the sinking of the *Herald of Free Enterprise* car ferry. The company had a history of bad industrial relations and working practices years before the disaster. At the enquiry indiscipline, weak management and drinking bouts were reported to be rife. The management had shortened the turn-round times of the roll-on, roll-off ferries, which meant that sometimes ferries put to sea in one of the world's busiest shipping lanes with their bow doors open – a dangerous practice. The design of the ships was such that the people on the bridge could not see if the bow doors had been closed, and there was no signalling system to tell them. Some members of the ship's crew felt obliged to write to the board asking for a simple signalling system. Their memo was returned to them struck through by a marker and with the word 'wimps' written across it. A few months later 193 people died when the very accident – involving open bow doors, a rough winter sea, six inches of water getting into the car deck and the ship capsizing – predicted by the crew occurred. Although there was an attempt to indict a board on the UK's first charge of corporate manslaughter, it was difficult to isolate the individuals responsible, and the potential charge became time expired.

Subsequently the first charge of corporate manslaughter in the UK, the OLL case in which a group of young children on a leisure holiday were knowingly put to sea in canoes in rapidly deteriorating weather conditions and died, has been prosecuted successfully and the managing director was jailed.

I realize that these are extreme examples, but I hope that they make the case that the values, attitudes and behaviours of directors and managers have a direct effect on the emotional climate of their organization, and, ultimately, on its subsequent performance.

Creating a Positive Emotional Climate

Once the issue of managing the emotional climate and processes is accepted by the directors and managers as a valid task which strengthens Organizational Capability, then many will admit that they do not know how to do anything about it.

After first ensuring that the purpose, vision and values are communicated and tested, it is crucial that the directors work with their managers to open up systems of continuous learning at the operational level – which will add meaning and challenge to people's day-to-day work (see pp. 11–14).

If the organization is well structured at the operational level an emotional climate will be created where avoidance of responsibility, non-acceptance of accountability, blaming others, withholding information and downright lying are broken as habits. All of these are highly corrosive of positive organizational values if allowed to become the norm, and must be challenged.

Three key attitudes and behaviours throughout the organization can continually reinforce the importance of Organizational Learning to the maintaining and development of the organization:

• Critical Review. The continuous and emotionally neutral ability to review critically policy, strategy, and operations.
• Continuing Dialogue. Ensures that environmental changes plus vision and values are prioritized against existing plans, and then communicated with feedback action learning.
• Action Learning. The total process of implementing priorities, strategy and plans, and ensuring feedback from the coal-face, is the key to the organization's learning.

The directors need to position the business brain (see p. 63) as the open forum of organizational debate and learning. This is key to creating a positive emotional climate. While directors are ultimately both accountable and responsible for their decisions and the consequences, and also for the design and control of the organizational learning process, they are not the only people in the organization who learn. Many staff members, customers and suppliers should be active in informing the continuing debate and decisions. Customer-facing staff are particularly important, as they are the most sensitive antennae for changing customer demand. Operations staff are vital as they carry out continuing critical review of the effectiveness and efficiency of the existing organizational processes, and so raise productivity. 'Whistle-blowers' are important in speaking out by reporting the breaking of the law and/or the values of the organization. Direction-givers and strategic thinkers are important in reframing the changing external environment, thus ensuring the organization's survival and effectiveness in its ecological niche.

None of this is particularly hard to achieve. However, systematic learning does need personal discipline, combined with effective organizational processes. Budgeting time for this is rarely a priority for most directors and line managers. Many believe that they cannot even afford just ten minutes a day to ask the four basic questions for line managers in a learning organizing (see p. 11).

The clear mapping of an organization's strengths and weaknesses, opportunities and threats, linked to critical review, continuous organizational dialogue and feedback from such powerful processes as action learning make a major contribution to Organizational Capability. When directors also attempt to ensure a positive emotional climate this can be the additional factor which takes them to superior performance.

But can we measure Organizational Capability? Is there a simple, unifying model which will give quantitative and qualitative information on both where the organization is at present, and where it needs to be in the future?

CHAPTER 6

The Twelve Elements of Organizational Capability

Until now I have stressed the interplay between organizational task and social-emotional processes. The challenge is now to create a unifying model to describe and measure the effect of both the formal and informal organizations on Organizational Capability, and to define a simple and consistent language of Organizational Capability.

So many organizations in the private and public fields are patently ineffective and inefficient to make such an attempt necessary. If we can begin to create a simple vocabulary, and some measures, of Organizational Capability, we will release a large amount of human energy and learning into a world where it is badly needed.

When I say 'a model', I am not asserting that the proposed twelve elements of Organizational Capability are totally predictive in themselves. At this stage in the development of organizational studies we are not dealing with an experimental science which seeks only laws, but with an interpretative science which searches for meaning. As seen in the references to complex adaptive systems, this may not be as 'soft' a mindset as it at first appears. Even 'hard' science is adapting and learning as the ideas of 'chaos' and 'complexity' become more accepted. Such concepts are useful in reflecting on the social-emotional interactions of individuals and groups, which are reinforced constantly by the organizational values, behaviours, language and symbols which have built up over time to create the organization's culture and brand.

AN INTRODUCTION TO THE ORGANIZATIONAL CAPABILITY MODEL

From a simple base in the late 1960s my wife Sally and I have developed the Organizational Capability model through our consulting and academic work. From an original six elements we have evolved a fuller model of twelve dimensions which is both necessary and sufficient to describe any organization and its capabilities. We found that if we added any more elements then the model tended to become uncontrollable and difficult to process, while if we used fewer elements, then we tended to miss the richness of the full picture. We are still experimenting with the number of elements needed to be sufficiently comprehensive without being overelaborate or redundant, but we have found that twelve elements are effective in describing organizations as different as a UK government department, a multinational electronic defence manufacturer and an architect's practice in Hong Kong.

Two ideas are key to our design:

- The basis for constructing an integrated and effective human organization must lie within the twelve elements.
- Each element must be *measurable* in quantitative and qualitative terms, thus demonstrating for each of the twelve dimensions the difference between where respondents (staff members, customers or suppliers) think the organization is, and where they feel it should be. This differential measure, or 'gap analysis', forms the basis of critical review of the organization, organizational dialogue, risk assessment and priority setting within the purpose, vision and values set by the directors.

For many years it has struck us as distinctly odd that bottom-line-driven directors and managers, people often fixated by numbers in the financial, production and service-delivery contexts, tend to go to pieces when faced with the idea of measuring the people and organizational aspects of their enterprise. Their belief that you cannot measure the 'soft' aspects of their organization, except in existing financial terms, means that crucial human data is never seen nor processed. This leads many organizations to have negative emotional climates, and I am sure that it causes most of the failures to implement strategy effectively which we have been asked to address as consultants.

Much of this is due to the absence of an organizational language or model within which directors can talk about their dilemmas. Not only is it impossible for them to do any gap analysis of Organizational Capability in this situation, but they are not even aware that it is possible. Yet the statistics to make the measurements have existed for many years: parametric statistics, (which every modern manager is taught) can be brought into play; and the less well-known non-parametric statistics which look at relativities, and relationships between items, rather than the basic quantum.

When faced with a major investment decision directors and managers will budget time to look carefully at their options, mutter chants about net present values, discount their project's cashflows, and make sensitivity analyses to assess risks. They are comfortable as they have both a language and an intellectual framework for doing so.

Yet if they are asked to make a similar set of assessments for a major organizational *change* – whether of a new structure, growth, merger, acquisition, repositioning, downsizing, or right-sizing etc. – they are usually mute, as they do not have the mind-set, or the tools, for this type of investment decision. There is no agreement about the relationship between people and capital and the likely consequences for both. For want of anything better this aspect of risk assessment is reluctantly handed over to the human resources department, usually not with the expectation of a useful response, but in hope of having someone to blame later. In reality organizations are all about relationships, formal or informal. They are living, inter-connected organisms, and can be both described and measured. The many directors who do not appreciate this in future must be considered organizationally illiterate.

What can be done about this? Again, it strikes me as odd that the standard answer is 'nothing', when so much has been known throughout history about the negative effects of organizational illiteracy, Gaius Petronius stated that:

> We trained hard ... but it seemed that every time we were beginning to form up in teams we would be reorganized. I was to learn later in life that we tend to meet any new situation by reorganizing, and a wonderful method it can be for creating the illusion of progress while producing confusion, inefficiency and demoralization.

This was written in AD 65, but so little has been achieved since then, that it could have been penned today.

THE ORGANIZATIONAL CAPABILITY MODEL

The twelve elements are:

1 Clarity of personal responsibility
2 Organizational clarity
3 Financial rewards
4 Personal rewards
5 Personal performance indicators
6 Group performance indicators
7 Work quality perspective
8 Competitor orientation
9 Organizational adaptiveness
10 Customer orientation
11 Leadership orientation
12 Learning climate

It cannot be said that an organization's strength or weakness in any of these areas will have guaranteed consequences in, say, three other areas, yet there is little doubt that each of the twelve elements inter-relate. They overlap in many ways, both in the formal organization, and informally, in people's heads. These relationships are so complex that the precise nature, or consequences, of each interaction cannot be predicted. Chance can play as great a part as design. Much is dependent on the relationship between the organization's changing external and internal environments, its espoused and informal structures, its learning processes, and the nature of the individuals and groups that define it at any moment. The paradox is that each of the twelve elements can be assessed through gap analysis.

The twelve elements can be displayed on two axes: Internal and External Focus; and Task and Emotional Process Focus. When combined these give the Organizational Capabilities quadrant:

	Internal Focus	External Focus
Task Focus		
Emotional Process Focus		

Figure 13 Framework for the Organizational Capability model

The Framework

This framework can be filled out by starting with the more internally focused, and task-focused, elements:

- Clarity of personal responsibility
- Organizational clarity
- Financial rewards

These are the 'hard', formal responsibilities of directors and managers, who need to ensure that effective systems are designed and monitored through critical review, via regular and rigorous feedback, for each of the three areas.

Then come the internally focused, emotional-process-focused, 'soft' elements, over which the individual has more control than the managers:

- Personal rewards
- Personal performance indicators
- Group performance indicators

These are formally the direct responsibilities of line managers and work-group leaders, but are informally driven by individuals or small groups. Effective and efficiently organized companies will build on this idea by increasingly positioning their line managers as coaches to work groups, to develop their members as individual knowledge workers.

The externally focused, and task-focused, 'hard' elements are:

- Work quality perspective
- Competitor orientation

Directors need to ensure that systems are installed by the managers and then rigorously monitored to give crucial, and often missed, data on this area. We can all be seduced easily by the urgency of present crises. Awareness of these 'hard' elements should help to prevent this dominating, by forcing a focus on the changing external environment.

The final part of the quadrant is completed by the externally focused and emotional-process-focused 'soft' elements of:

- Organizational adaptiveness
- Customer orientation

The ability of individual and work groups to empathize with changing customer needs and immediate problems, while responding to changing external environments, is the sign of a healthy organization.

The four quadrants alone are not sufficient to create a model because they have no dynamic or energy. The integration of the whole into a living, capable, organism comes from two meta-elements:

- Leadership orientation
  and
- Learning climate

	Internal Focus	External Focus
Task Focus	• Clarity of Personal Responsibility • Organizational Clarity • Financial Rewards	• Work Quality Perspective • Competitor Orientation
	→ Leadership Orientation ┐ └ Learning Climate ←	
Emotional Process Focus	• Personal Rewards • Personal Performance Indicators • Group Performance Indicators	• Organizational Adaptiveness • Customer Orientation

Figure 14 The Twelve Organizational Capabilities model

Directors and senior managers have a difficult role in that they must drive the enterprise forwards while keeping it under prudent control. The classic directoral dilemma is how to spend time thinking about the future and showing the way ahead, while simultaneously trying to keep the present in order. This is a task element of the highest order which, paradoxically, is achieved through continuing, 'soft', learning processes. The directors must also ensure sufficient social-emotional lubrication to allow the tasks to be carried out effectively as well as efficiently. This is best done by nurturing a positive attitude to organizational learning – the learning climate. Only by this can Organizational Capability and the organization's responsiveness within its ecological niche be enhanced. Here we are trying to address the frequent organizational 'shadow side' behaviour of spending significant time and money in *not* learning – hiding mistakes, sweeping them under the carpet, and, if found out, blaming others whilst refusing to accept responsibility for our actions.

One final reminder on the Organizational Capability quadrant. The task elements – internal and external – reflect the main areas of control and motivational influence over the organization by the

		Internal Focus	Exteral Focus
Areas of maximum influence by the organization	Task Focus		
Areas of maximum influence by the individual	Emotional Process Focus		

Figure 15 Areas of influence over Organizational Capability

directors and managers. The emotional process element – internal and external – are the main areas of control and influence over the organization by the individual. Both task and emotional process are vital in ensuring a capable organization.

The benefits, and the added value consequences, of this integration of the twelve elements of Organizational Capability are usually missed by organizationally illiterate directors and managers. They are becoming key competencies of effective twenty-first-century directors and managers.

Internal, Task-Focused Elements

1. CLARITY OF PERSONAL RESPONSIBILITY

Most people do not know exactly what their jobs are. This bald statement is the distillation of some twenty years of interviewing people at all levels in organizations in many parts of the world. It only takes a few moments' thought to realize why this unsatisfactory situation exists – most people get a job description at the start of a job. This is never revised, and ends up bearing little resemblance to reality. A few companies are now doing away with job descriptions, because they believe that they are unsuited to the realities of modern organizations, and do not reflect environmental and structural changes rapidly enough.

Job descriptions are comforting. They are the sheet anchor with which people try to hold their positions in the turbulent seas of modern organizational life. They are reassuring in that they form the basis of the legal contract of employment. This contract, at least in civil societies, enables individuals to go to a court of justice or a tribunal if they feel that they have been badly or criminally treated. The fact that individuals know the precise specifications of their work – the clarity of personal responsibility – and the legal basis on which they are contracted has served both organizations and individuals well until recently.

However, there are two clear ways in which such clarity is being undermined. First, if line managers, or work-group leaders, are not obliged by their job description to coach new recruits through the essential and sequential processes of induction, inclusion and competence building, then one often finds an opaqueness, rather than a clarity of personal responsibility.

The induction process explains to an individual the 'hard' technical tasks – what their work is, what the volume and quality targets are, how the reward and benefits systems work, what the Health and Safety at Work procedures are, and what the formal organizational rules are. Induction is usually handled well, if a little mechanically, in most organizations until the senior manager and executive levels are reached, where it evaporates. There seems to be a global conspiracy to ensure that no time or money budgets are allocated to these crucial activities at these levels and beyond. Directors especially are assumed to be omniscient!

The inclusion process is more subtle, and often ignored by line managers keen on hitting targets and getting great bottom lines quickly. But it is essential if clarity of personal responsibility is to be achieved. Inclusion is the key 'soft' process by which an individual quickly and effectively becomes an active member of a work group. This applies as much to a member of the board of directors as to a part-time security guard. It does not have to be an overtly 'hearts on sleeves' process. If a line manager spends five to ten minutes a day coaching a newcomer through both the induction to tasks and the social integration processes, and so demonstrates to the work group the additional energy and diversity that he or she brings, then the competence of that individual can be developed quickly, creating both a financial and social return on this investment. If this is not done then at some point over the first six to nine weeks the new entrant is likely to be distanced socially from the work group. This does not mean that they will be fully excluded, rather that they will rarely be fully included. They will be left in an organizational limbo, a form of purgatory, from which they are unlikely ever to emerge while they remain with that work group. Despite being a 'soft', social-emotional process, inclusion has 'hard' characteristics, as without both induction and inclusion, task achievement is difficult, if not impossible. A new member may fit the job description perfectly, and have all the technical skills needed and more, but without the emotional acceptance of their work group they cannot fully exercise their competences. Inclusion is work-group specific. It is essential that line managers and personnel specialists understand and use this fact when they design organizational structures and processes.

The form and process of inclusion will depend as much on the individual as the line manager, although the line manager must be held responsible for its occurrence. Inclusion can be blatant or subtle. It can be gentle, or involve bizarre ceremonies. It can mean socializing with the work group for relaxation, joining their sporting activities, or on acceptance into certain clubs or societies. My father was included into the world of the master engraver on completing his printing apprenticeship at the end of the Second World War by being tarred and feathered and rolled in a barrel down Fleet Street. This was considered a great honour – it was a sign that he had stopped being a boy, and was now a journeyman. Nowadays, such 'inclusion' would be seen as criminal assault.

In East Asia the chairman of a massive company kept his board under control by giving some, but never all, of his directors one of his home-made cheeses each Christmas. The directors were all very rich and could easily have bought as many cheeses as they would ever need in their lives, but that was not the point. The real issue was, who did the chairman recognize as having done good work that year? Who was *included*? The directors were unnaturally acquiescent during the three months before Christmas. The chairman exercised his power during this time by putting his particular policies and strategies onto the board agenda, knowing that few, if any, would oppose them. The directors all wished to be included. This example also gives some insight into the typically opaque nature of directors' personal responsibility, and their confused role perception, in this international company.

Similarly, in a UK company I was invited to work with a board, and at its first meeting a young director, who had, significantly, been on the board for two years, was presented with a small piece of card. He was delighted, they were delighted, and I could not see what was on the card. It turned out to be a season ticket for their directors' box at, unfortunately, Spurs football club. Inclusion was not so much about who was on the board, but who was invited to sit in the directors' box.

Perversely, clarity of personal responsibility can be used as a weapon against organizational integration, especially in some hierarchical corporate and national cultures. Job specifications and job evaluations in such cultures specify precisely not only what is to be done, but also what is not to be done. For personal health, safety and quality reasons this can be wise. It would, for example, be unwise for an airline engineer to put more torque on an engine bolt than was specified by a manufacturer, or for a bank manager to exceed his lending limit, or for a board to exceed its reserved powers and its articles of association.

All of these things happen, but if the organizational structure and emotional climate is essentially bureaucratic, then sticking strictly to a job description is the key to organizational survival. It is a common complaint that bureaucracies are customer-unfriendly and unable to flex to specific needs. This is their nature, and in order to change it the structure, values and mind-set, social processes and emotional climate must be changed. This is usually too daunting a prospect for any individual. So would-be change-agents either group together to take political action: e.g., privatizing a government department so that it has to be both financially and customer accountable; or they take individual action in the external environment to influence the informal organization. There are three basic ways to change a bureaucrat's mind through the informal organization:

- The threat, or use, of physical force
- The use of family or personal connections
- The illegal passing of bribes

In many 'developing' countries a culture has grown up which blends elements of all three into an art form for getting anything done at all. In such countries people feel that they have no possibility of changing the unresponsive formal structures. Their job descriptions, or job assumptions, most certainly do not allow for any such thing. Many Western businessmen pour scorn on this, complaining bitterly about the need to break down such unhelpful bureaucracies, and demanding the immediate creation of a civil society underpinned by 'the rule of law'. They often forget that it takes at least two parties for corruption to exist. In Germany a bribe paid abroad is tax deductible, and in certain cases in the UK this is also the case. Unresponsive bureaucracies will not be keen to reform so long as the West has double standards about such issues.

Even in 'developed' Europe and the US we still face bureaucratic issues, as anyone who has tried to deal, for example, with a national personal taxation office will find. Doing business in Italy, Spain or, in particular, France and Belgium, can lead the unwary into bureaucratic nightmares where you seem to tread the endless corridors of Kafka's *Castle* in a fruitless search for someone who can take the decision you need in order to achieve your aim. Each functionary has remarkable clarity of personal responsibility, and never seems to be able to deal with your particular need – they are either too low, or too high, in the hierarchy to take this decision. They are explicit about what they can and, especially, what they cannot do, because it is spelled out in the rules, to which you are never given access.

The late James Cameron, journalist and war correspondent, told a wonderfully insightful story about the nature of bureaucracies, job descriptions and their powers, and of discriminating questioning. He had a recurrent nightmare in which he got trapped in a cold climate wearing only tropical clothes. He made frequent trips to North Vietnam during the Vietnam War. Travelling in and out was not easy, and he had to take some curious routes on even curiouser airlines. On one flight out of Hanoi the aeroplane ran into trouble and was diverted to Maoist Beijing. He had no visa for China, and the immigration official gave him a hard time by refusing to exercise his discretionary powers. He said that James could not enter the country, but neither could he leave, because he did not have an exit visa. Cameron asked what he should do. The official replied that he would have to get a taxi into town – a long journey in those days – and try to get an exit visa, but it would be difficult as he spoke no Putonghua, and only two and a half hours remained before the offices closed for the weekend. Clad in tropical clothes in a freezing climate he set off on a Kafkaesque journey through the halls of the Ministry of Immigration. After hours of fruitless search he did not succeed, and returned to the airport completely frozen, depressed and unable to think what he should do next. In despair, and furious, he was taken to see the same official who had interviewed him earlier. Eventually the official spoke. 'The problem is of your own making, Mr Cameron. When you arrived you asked "What should I do?" It would have been wiser to ask "What would you do?"' He then stamped the passport with an exit visa.

Away from bureaucracies, those without a job description will define their job for themselves. This can work very well if they do so in close co-operation with the organization's vision and values, particularly in smaller organizations, where the need for high levels of adaptiveness demand the self-management of job descriptions and role perceptions, but in large organizations such self-management presents a problem for line managers. It is a key part of the line manager's work to ensure that job descriptions and the subsequent clarity of personal responsibility are checked regularly, and adapted quickly when circumstances change, to ensure organizational survival.

2. ORGANIZATIONAL CLARITY

Organization charts, which are meant to map the way the corporation works, as we have seen, often bear little relationship to the everyday reality of working life.

Most begin with the managing director, or chief executive officer. By doing so they avoid the issue of the relationship between ownership, power, authority, responsibility and ultimate accountability – the board and corporate governance issues. This means that organization charts are seen by the vast majority of people purely as a rough map of the operations of the company. This is usually laid out on paper as a classic pyramidal hierarchy, with the managing director at the top and the humblest form of organizational life at the bottom. Little regular critical review of the organization chart is done by directors, who frequently do not even appear on the chart and are not encouraged by the chairman to ask such intelligently naive questions as: 'Does this structure reflect the reality of the organization at present?'; and 'What is the basic organizational design mix: classic pyramid, inverted pyramid, arrowhead, centre/periphery, matrix, federation, learning organization, or complex adaptive system?', and 'What is the most appropriate structure for our changing future?'

If the chart does not reflect the organization clearly, then what can be done to ensure that the vertical and horizontal – the power and integration – relationships are clarified? One way is to ensure that senior managers are charged with reporting regularly to the board on the evolving organization structure and processes, and its appropriateness. This can be started with a simple survey which lists for each part of the organization:

- Main tasks
- Subsidiary tasks
- Levels of authority (derived in association with the board's reserved powers)
- 'Dotted line' relationships
- Areas of friction with other departments, and options for improvement
- Areas of activity missing in either the vertical or horizontal information and work flows

This critical review is just a simple managerial task, yet it is rarely done with any regularity or rigour. I believe that this is due mainly to a lack of awareness among directors for the need for it. Such review is crucial in order to ensure a level of continuing organizational clarity, and hence, optimize productivity.

Surprisingly few induction programmes take an individual through the complete manufacturing or service delivery process, not just talking them through the organization chart, but also walking them through the physical organization. Without such an induction it is much more difficult to respond to the vertical and horizontal relationships in the organization, and the changing demands they make of each other. If this is not done, then an emotional climate develops which makes people more inward-looking, potentially hostile to other departments, and willing to hide mistakes and blame others.

To improve organizational clarity it must first be ensured that the induction documents accurately reflect the organizational model which directors and senior managers have designed, and wish to maintain. Second, the interconnectedness of each work group, department and division must be both described and critically reviewed regularly and transparently for all staff. They will need to see not just such outputs as their work volumes and quality standards, but the effect they have on the volume and quality of the work of others.

This notion of 'transparent' work-group measurement – where all staff are aware of input, throughput and output data – is beginning to grow rapidly as organizations accept that they must be more integrated and adaptive. Models such as:

- Service/Profit Chain
- Value Chains
- Balanced Scorecards
- European Foundation for Quality Management 'Business Excellence' model

are designed to address this problem and will be covered in more detail in the next chapter.

Each model stresses the need for organizational clarity and the interconnectedness of modern organizations. These pressures will grow as we enter the twenty-first century.

3. FINANCIAL REWARDS

This is usually the most controversial of all organizational issues, and presents a classic dilemma for directors and senior managers. It seems to be part of the human condition that everybody wants to be in the 'top quartile' for their company or industry. If an organization does pay in the upper quartile, then a very good case has to be made, both to the increasingly critical shareholders and, in many countries, to national governments, but if pay falls in the bottom quartile, then staff usually feel uncomfortable. Across the world it has been a given that employees in public service would trade off lower financial rewards for the guarantee of continuing employment, but in today's uncertain world, even this promise of job security can be in doubt.

In the UK in the 1960s and 1970s the 'differentials' game was played frequently and successfully by the trades unions. They realized quickly that, as there was never a single, long-term, benchmark 'market rate', the whole system could be driven quite quickly to absurdity. Each worker group tried to leapfrog the others 'to maintain our differentials' and threatened industrial action if they were denied. Once this vicious cycle has started it can raise labour rates to such a level that manufacturers and service deliverers are forced out of markets, redundancies grow rapidly, the taxation system starts to underfund the public sector, redundancies occur there, and the vicious cycle reinforces itself until the markets exert their 'invisible hand'.

A similar cycle appears to be under way with directors, senior managers, professionals and financial traders who claim with increasing ferocity, but decreasing credibility, that they are rare resources for which the market price is always rising. This is patently absurd, and will inevitably end in tears, as the economics of an organization cannot stand this for long, and the social effects cause public concern and political action. In the UK the public spotlight is at present rightly on the 'fat cats' of industry, especially those in the newly privatized sectors. In Indonesia, Thailand, Malaysia, the Philippines, South Korea, Japan and Russia we see examples of the system taken to its ultimate absurdity as 'crony capitalism', or 'gangster capitalism', creates similar vicious cycles of overpayment and then collapse.

Financial rewards must be linked to individual and total corporate performance at all levels. A truly values-based appraisal system, linked with an integrated organizational model such as the EFQM Business Excellence model, can make all the difference, because everyone can see their inputs and outputs and agree the appropriate financial rewards.

In the *Through the Looking Glass* world of financial rewards, current models tend to be linked to performance-related pay in the short term. Sadly, much of this performance-related pay is linked to simple output volumes rather than profitability, or, even better, productivity. The latter would certainly help the long-term health of the organization, but at present most schemes only allow directors and managers to juggle the short-term figures. The saying that 'there is nothing more dangerous for the continuing health of an organization than a 60 year old CEO with a stock option' rings horribly true. However, a few organizations are facing up to this and insisting that all performance-related bonuses are geared to the medium and long term. Any contractually agreed bonus system is broken into three elements. One third is paid on the achievement of the bonus at the end of a financial year. Two thirds of the bonus are held over. The next third is paid at the end of the following financial year only if organizational performance is maintained or improved. The final third is paid at the end of the third year, under the same conditions as year two. Such a system attempts to keep directors' and managers' minds on sustainable improvements, while reducing their propensity to change jobs quickly.

A separate issue occurs when directors' and senior managers' financial rewards are pegged by shareholder or government actions. This can be demoralizing for staff, who can then see no way of raising their financial rewards or other benefits despite any improvement in their performance.

Herzberg's classic slogan 'hygiene is not enough' (see pp. 71–3), seems to hold true in both public and private organizations. Indeed, in the public sector, where pay and conditions are often negotiable only within very tight limits, my wife and I frequently find that financial rewards are the number one issue. However, most staff recognize that significant change is not usually achievable on this aspect, certainly in the short term. They accept, albeit grudgingly, that within the strong ethos of public service a mixture of the benefit of more job security, blended with the satisfaction of doing a socially responsible job well, and being recognized for it, must outweigh the financial rewards. They still complain about their financial rewards but rely on getting their personal rewards elsewhere.

Internal, Emotional-process-focused Elements

4. PERSONAL REWARDS

Even if staff are unhappy with their financial rewards they often get rewards elsewhere – in personal job satisfaction. Recognition for a good job as an individual, or group, is the apex of most people's existence at work – it is the key to personal rewards and satisfaction. We spend so much time at work, that despite the rhetoric of the IT industry (whatever happened to the much-hyped 'leisure society'?), recognition is often the main driver for our emotional satisfaction. People crave recognition, and it is the line manager's job to ensure that they get it, starting with the induction, inclusion and competence-building process, and continuing through values-based appraisals and personal development plans until a job change or retirement.

Positive recognition of aspects such as the achievement of volume and quality targets, project milestones, customer satisfaction targets, supplier chain targets etc. are essential to sustain people's energy and enthusiasm for their work. Personal recognition can be as simple as the line manager giving an authentic 'thank you'. Curiously, many line managers throughout the world feel that saying thank you is beneath them. They feel that it demeans them, and that the staff should be thankful for the fact that they are being paid – that is thought to be satisfaction enough for anyone. It is not. Why should not a few seconds of line managers' time be given to personal recognition when it is due? Without it there can be serious consequences. The reason is very simple. If people do not get positive personal recognition, then the one thing that a human being cannot stand at all is no recognition, and will, if forced, seek negative recognition by deliberately committing errors. No recognition signifies that either they are not seen to exist, or that they have no part to play in the organization. So, rather than having no recognition, most people would prefer, just, to have *negative* recognition. Therefore, they make mistakes, ignore or forget instructions, frequently take time off as 'sick', and exhibit signs of organizational indiscipline and lack of self-control. Their 'reward' is to be heavily criticized negatively, to be shouted at, abused, cussed and generally reviled – but at least they are recognized. How much is your Personal Rewards system based on negative rather than positive recognition?

The area of personal development opportunities is also important. If a personal development plan is built into the appraisal and continuing professional development process, then this focus on an individual's long-term employability helps enormously in creating a positive emotional climate in the organization. This reinforces the link to another of the 'soft', internally orientated/social-emotional aspects of Organizational Capability – Personal Performance Indicators.

5. PERSONAL PERFORMANCE INDICATORS

This element of Organizational Capability builds on aspects of both clarity of personal responsibilities and personal rewards. Without clarity, and specified levels of authority in the individual's job description, it is impossible to assess accurately an individual's performance. Yet the vast majority of people I meet in organizations are unclear as to how their personal performance is actually measured. There are often few agreed benchmarks or targets.

It is at this point that the 'hard' tasks and 'soft' processes meet head-to-head. Clarity about both *what* targets will be met and by whom, and *how* the process of achieving them will be carried out is essential. To achieve this a system of regular and rigorous assessment which covers each person in the organization, and gives equal weight to task achievement and values-based behaviours must be in place.

It is not enough to measure solely task achievement. There is a slowly growing awareness amongst many directors and managers of a causal and qualitative connection between task achievement and the lubricating effects of social process. This will become more important as we move into the 'knowledge worker' organizations of the twenty-first century. Companies at the leading edge are beginning to reorganize their appraisal systems so that they reflect and reward a maximum of fifty per cent of the whole for task achievement, and a maximum of fifty per cent for the organizational values-based behaviours that achieved the tasks. Both the what and the how are given equal weight.

As mentioned, the organizational values must be turned into two or three specific behaviours which reflect aspects of each value. If an organizational value is openness, then the assessable behaviours might be 'admitting mistakes quickly to other members of the work group', or 'noticing others' problems and offering help', or 'being seen to keep an open mind when change is suggested'.

Two things are important to hold in mind in relation to personal performance indicators. First, carefully selected and tested values, and the consequent assessable behaviours, directly affect the emotional climate and so the long-term culture of an organization. For clues as to the real values of the organization, staff will watch carefully the directors and senior managers to see if they really 'talk the talk'. If their actions do not align with their espowsed values, then the staff will always follow the behaviours rather than the rhetoric. It is in their interests to do so because these are likely to be the true measures of personal performance.

Sadly, failure to talk the talk creates an emotional climate of scepticism, leading over time to downright cynicism. For example, the directors' much vaunted 'quality excellence programme' might be undermined by their reluctance to check frequently the quality of output. In manufacturing the acid test is often what is loaded on to the trucks on a Friday afternoon at the end of the Western working week. Surprising lapses in quality excellence are often allowed to occur in an attempt to reach the volume targets. By using a values-based appraisal system regularly, remarkably good results can be obtained, because it is impossible to attain more than half of a positive assessment on task achievement alone. Effective personal performance demands effectiveness in social-emotional processes, although an excessively 'touchy feely' approach can mean a lack of focus on task achievement which can be equally disabling.

Second, the growing trend is towards not just values-based appraisal but also to linking this to feedback from others at appraisal time: 'upward feedback', '360 degree feedback', 'peer assessment' etc. These are designed to blend and expand task and social process achievements.

Upward feedback is a system for appraising each staff member on previously agreed criteria. The boss assesses staff individually, while each of them assesses the boss. The key idea is to see how the boss can help his or her employees to achieve their tasks more effectively, and vice versa. This can be an eye-opener, as many blockages previously thought unmentionable within, and between, work groups are made transparent. This needs careful handling initially and the use of a facilitator is strongly recommended. If the feedback is then handled constructively – using such open questions as 'How can I improve . . . ?' rather than the closed and initially disabling question 'Why did you say . . . ?' – it can make a significant difference to the relations between a boss and their work group, so creating a constructive emotional temperature in the work group and, ultimately, in the total organization.

For example, when working with boards I have built up a level of trust through sharing such peer feedback – the process is simple. There is a flip-chart sheet for each board member with the words 'Stop', 'Start' and 'Continue' written on it. The participants are then left plenty of time to fill in, individually, their needs of each other board member specifically to:

- Stop doing things that block their colleague's ability to work effectively.
- Start doing things that will better use their colleague's talents and aspirations.
- Continue doing the things that really help their colleague.

There is then usually a long and quiet period where people read their own sheets and ponder the meaning of them. After that there is an even longer period where they come together to discuss the meaning of the words written, and the emotions expressed, before getting agreement on how they will try to work together in future, and how this will be monitored. Again, the use of a facilitator is strongly recommended.

A constructive focus on assessing task and social process achievement is not as Orwellian as many managers fear. It does not attempt to change a person's personality, or thoughts, only their behaviours and in a constructive way which will help both individuals and their work group achieve targets more effectively and efficiently.

Three hundred and sixty degree feedback builds on the notions of upward, or peer, feedback, but does it in heroic style. The system gathers comments from the individual being assessed, their direct reports, their peers and their boss, about their task performance and the appropriateness of their behaviours in relation to organizational values. In some cases, even customers and suppliers become part of the appraisal process. It is a very rich source of information which allows good understanding of the issues and, therefore, the ability to plan subsequent actions well. But it takes a lot of time to process the resulting data and to turn it into information – if directors and managers budget time effectively this should not cause difficulties, but most do not, and in such circumstances 360 degree feedback can quickly get a bad name as an overly bureaucratic system. Learning is required to run it efficiently. I usually introduce an upward feedback system first and let people learn how to use it over a year. If it is then working well, we can move on to peer assessment as well. By this time most of the staff are keen to be involved, and it has a very positive effect on the emotional climate of the organization, especially if the players are involved in the design and development of the system from the beginning. As an example, I was asked to facilitate the upward feedback process at the very top of a financial services company. They had designed their own model, with some twenty measurable elements for appraisal which revolved around task achievement and the appropriate social-emotional processes to back them. My client was overall head of the international company, with some twelve direct reports who had completed their part of the upward feedback survey. I was initially briefed on the system by its designers, a group of senior managers and the human resources division head. Then, my client and I went over his personal feedback in some depth on three occasions over a week, before he decided that he was ready to face his direct reports. The pattern of feedback was remarkably similar – he was seen as extraordinarily successful in task achievement but could be emotionally abrasive in his work processes (specific examples were given), and this was seen to block some vital information about both the business and its people from him. The meeting with his direct reports allowed him to say to them that he recognized the problems, and asked for answers. These did not come easily at first, but after some time his direct reports opened up, and an agreed personal development plan was created which would be monitored by his boss – the company chairman.

The fact that 'the old man' had actually put himself through the process had a very positive effect on the total organization – few believed that he would do it, let alone that he would have a personal development plan which would be monitored. He even wrote an article about the process in the company newspaper to reinforce this point.

The fact that even the old man could change led to much debate throughout the organization, particularly as to what the company's values should be in future. To begin with, the executive directors were surveyed on their views of the espoused values, and they were split equally between those who rated 'increasing shareholder value' as the priority, and those who rated 'achieving customer satisfaction' first. Rather than accept one dominant value we adopted a 'both . . . and' approach, and promoted awareness of this 'values dilemma' – how to increase shareholder value through improving customer satisfaction?

The values suggested by the staff are now being assessed, and there is a guarantee from the directors that they will be built into the selection process, the appraisal system, and the training and development processes. This will take time, probably five years, to work through the total organization. The good news is that by clarifying the personal performance indicators in terms of task *and* process achievement the emotional temperature of the company is beginning to warm noticeably. Admittedly, it was near freezing point at the start, but it is at least now tepid and should be at body heat within a few years. I count this as a remarkable transformation.

6. GROUP PERFORMANCE INDICATORS

Using a combined task achievement and values-based behavioural appraisal system, work groups can be assessed in ways similar to individuals. Unfortunately in many organizations, work groups are assessed only on their task achievement. This inevitably leads to a range of negative emotions, and blocked organizational learning that characterizes so many work groups around the world.

However, the growing movement to see work groups not as single, autonomous units, but as parts of an integrated whole – back to the original meaning of 'organization' – is creating new issues surrounding the measurement of work-group performance.

Two major factors seem to be converging to redefine work-group performance indicators. First, the growing awareness of the importance of the customers' and consumers' emotionally driven perception of the organization's effectiveness and efficiency. Work on understanding, highlighting and then taking action, to create as positive a perception as possible, is now under way in many organizations in relation to external customers. These are the people who pay money for the product or service, or, the consumer who use the product or service for which others have paid, e.g., the community services provided by local government.

Second, 'internal customers and consumers' are now being recognized as important. At present, most are consumers in the terms given above rather than true money-paying customers.

The group performance indicators include the specified delivery to:

- Quality
- Time
- Budget

Increasingly these indicators are also being linked into such systems as:

- Customer care and satisfaction
- Just in time delivery
- Quality of inter-team working; or 'service delivery agreements'

Here the inter-relationships, particularly at the boundaries between work groups, are being measured more sensitively. The excellent work of Deming, Juran and Revans in developing such measurement systems is increasingly being used for this – belated recognition for three very individualistic nonagenarian statisticians.

Such numeric data has an emotional dimension which is often overlooked. The regular monitoring by senior managers of basic group health and effectiveness indicators can throw new light onto the assessment of group performance. Such indicators would profile:

- The member's length of time with the organization
- The member's length of time in their present job
- Sickness rate
- Absenteeism rate
- Job turnover rate
- Accident rate
- Levels of assessed competences
- Personal development achievements

All of these are very easy and cheap to collect, process and review. In many companies their collection is part of line managers' job descriptions. Critical analysis of both these 'softer' measures, and the other 'harder' measures given above, can help identify quickly blocks in the flow process of work through the organization.

Whether it is a problem with materials handling or customer perception, or an unacceptably high rate of sickness in a work group, the group performance indicators are key managerial tools which can encourage continuous learning and adaptation in the organization. The director's job is to ensure that the systems for supervising management, and their creation of a positive emotional climate, are in place.

External, Task-focused Elements

7. WORK QUALITY PERSPECTIVE

It follows naturally from the group performance indicators that a constant flow of feedback from customers and/or consumers is crucial to ensuring product or service quality and so continuing profitability. In any organization there is an ever-present tension between the work groups' perception of the reality of their output in terms of quantity and quality, and the customers' perception at the receiving end.

Measuring the gap between these two perceptions is a continuous managerial process. This means regularly surveying both customers' and consumers' perceptions to gain an external view, and the work-group inputs and outputs to gain an internal measure. The resulting figures are the gap analysis. Customer satisfaction surveys alone are not enough, although they do allow the customer's changing perception of what is good-value-for-money in your products or services to be checked constantly. Creating this perception of good-value-for-money so that you are clearly differentiated in a customer's mind from your competitors, that means they will pay a premium price – the golden goal of most organizations. Few reach it.

The 'hard' side of work quality, from the directors' and managers' point of view, lies in ensuring two goals. First, that there are systems installed and maintained for spotting and correcting errors, and for learning continuously from them. To achieve this the learning climate of the organization needs to be one of openness, or transparency: it needs the willingness to admit mistakes quickly; assess risks; take corrective actions; and inform others on either side of the group's work-flow.

Second, an emotional climate of continuous improvement needs to be created. The work of Deming, Juran and Revans shows how to measure such progress using an essentially statistical base. Revans then went further and looked at the social-emotional systems of learning which operate around the hard data.[31] Continuous improvement allows quite small steps to be taken which, aggregated over time, lead to significant improvements. If large jumps in improvement are demanded immediately, then the Organizational Capabilities are often not there to deliver them, but work groups trained in continuous, 'action-learning' techniques can deliver more effectively major changes in the design, manufacture and service delivery cycles which simultaneously greatly improve both the emotional climate and organizational culture.

To achieve both goals, the emotional climate needs to be such that the reasons for change are not seen to be mean-minded or bottom-line obsessed. If the 'push for quality' is really only a way of improving profitability while stripping out the customer's and staff's perceived benefits of your product or service, then once again, actions fail to measure up to the rhetoric. Improving quality while reducing cost is the aim of thoughtful directors and managers. The cost improvements need to be 'customer invisible', so that they do not feel antagonized by yet another organization promising big improvements, but actually delivering less for the same price. The banks' service centres and the airlines' code-sharing mentioned before are good examples of this.

Ensuring customer satisfaction with high work quality often means having to set up pilot projects to demonstrate the new systems in operation, while openly learning how to improve them continuously. Pilot projects are a good way of easing quickly organizational opposition to change. The classic 'negative to positive' change cycle can help understanding here:

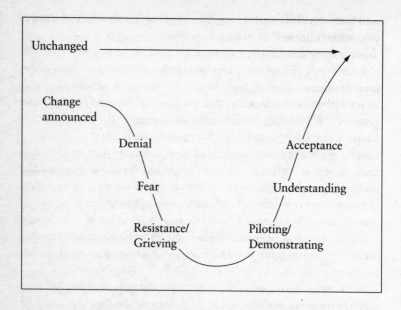

Figure 16 Unblocking resistance to change

8. COMPETITOR ORIENTATION

How much attention do you pay to, and how much information do you have on, your competitors? We are often surprised when carrying out our Organizational Capabilities survey to find that many organizations never seriously, and regularly, consider their competitors. This includes public sector bodies, which may not be competing for customers but are competing for scarce resources.

Organizations may have rather fuzzy, over-comfortable notions of their 'industry formula' – the generally accepted context, ways of delivering product or service, and terms of trade which seem common for that market sector. In any sector there is always much folklore and myth surrounding the nature of the opposition and your positioning in relation to them. But where is the hard information? Systematic monitoring of the external environment so that you are aware of your competitors' strengths and weaknesses, their changing opportunities and threats, their aspirations and plans, and from this data can benchmark all twelve elements of Organizational Capability, is often considered unnecessary, and rather unsporting. In a global economy it is vital.

I am not talking of industrial espionage. There is no need to employ undercover agents, spy techniques, telephone taps and other illegal methods to achieve a good perspective on your competitors'. The sources of public information are many. If you know what you are looking for, then regular and rigorous scanning of trade and professional journals, attendance at conferences and trade exhibitions, and careful reading of your competitors' annual reports and accounts, press statements and interviews will give you a wealth of data – most of it free. The skill is in using and interpreting this information, so developing an Organizational Capability in this area. The aim is to get people at all levels, especially the customer-facing staff and their supervisors, so sensitive to changing customer demands and the competitors' responses, that they see it as a vital part of their work to collect such data and feed it upwards. Directors must install feedback systems so that they can take wise strategic decisions to keep their customers, staff and shareholders happy.

Such activity and sensitivity can easily be built into job descriptions and appraisal systems. Customer-facing staff can be trained to ask simple questions about changing demand, through their talking with the customers and the competitors, and then to feed this back quickly to their supervisors for debate with the managers and directors. Executives can be trained to scan the media regularly, as part of their normal work, so that they are increasingly aware of changes in the external world and their competitors' changing relationship to them. None of this costs much money, and all of it can be time-budgeted as part of a normal working week. However, it does take self-discipline.

All levels of the organization can be encouraged to record regularly what they are learning about competitors, in the same way that they record information about customers. This data needs to be available at a central point, where competitor analysis is focused. This analysis should then be available within the intranet, so that the direction-givers and marketers are best able to position the organization's scarce resources to achieve its purpose, visions and values.

It is the mark of a healthy organization to have developed a cost-effective competitor analysis process to keep it ahead of the competition. This helps build up confidence and Organizational Capability. Such information will have additional value as projects become global, or just bigger and more complex. Increasingly few organizations will have all the resources needed even to qualify to tender for major works. Companies will increasingly need to learn to co-operate on specific projects with their competitors, while still competing with them elsewhere. Such 'co-opetition' is already becoming common in the design, executive coaching and multi-media worlds. My company Media Projects International has a project-based joint venture in East Asia with one of its competitors. We are not big enough to tender separately for the projects but by pooling our joint resources we were, and we won. Yet we still compete for other projects. There are growing numbers of examples elsewhere.

External, Emotional-process Focused Elements

9. ORGANIZATIONAL ADAPTIVENESS

In a fast-changing world a key Organizational Capability, perhaps *the* key Organizational Capability, is the speed at which an enterprise can learn to change. Changes in the external environment in terms of customer needs, competitor positioning, political policies, physical environmental laws, and economic and societal trends must be responded to if the organization is to survive and develop. The rate at which the organization's learning responds to the rate of change determines the level of its Organizational Capability. Does your organization have sufficient nimbleness, and organizational learning systems, to respond? Or is it lumbering, like a short-sighted rhinoceros, towards the cliff edge?

Before launching major organizational change it is wise to remember that there will be some people who will not need to participate. It is crucial to identify them and to protect them as much as possible from the physical and emotional change processes which will be affecting all the others. These 'stability factor' people are the bedrock which will enable the organization to continue functioning while changes occur around them. They are fundamental to customer perceptions during this turbulent time, yet most organizational change processes that I have seen do not bother to identify or protect such people. This often has calamitous effects when they get sucked unnecessarily into the fear and resistance stages of change.

It is part of the human condition to react with a degree of negativity to any proposed change. Normally people will first deny that change is needed, or happening. They will then go into fear mode for a period which could last for minutes or months, depending on the nature and speed of the change. There follows a period of conscious or unconscious resistance, often associated with a debilitating period of grieving for the past. This is especially true in organizations which have made many people redundant. Here the resistance can also take the form of grief for those who have gone. Such grieving can go on for months, as the survivors miss their lost colleagues and ask 'Why was I kept on instead of them?'

I was recently in a company which has been through wave after wave of downsizing over four years, talking to a senior manager who was looking worn out and ill. I asked him why this was so, as he had been appointed to the top job in his division. He replied that he was shot through. He had been asked to reapply for his own job five times in those four years. This had completely unnerved him and his family, who kept assuming that he would be made redundant, and who had to keep making appropriate plans to continue, for example, the children's education. He had lost all confidence in, and loyalty to, the company, despite having achieved a significant rewards package. He said that although he had the top job he wasn't really energized to do it, and there were others like him at his level. Sadly, thoughtless bottom-line improvement exercises frequently cause this, resulting in the loss of focus on work quality. Pilot projects which demonstrate future quality and quantity needs can begin to show a picture of the likely future while many staff are still in the negative stages of change. To ensure work quality this very emotionally sensitive period needs to be carefully managed. The positive aspects can be emphasized by using enthusiastic volunteer action-learning teams – volunteers who work in small, multidisciplinary, problem-solving groups of around six people, learning by combining analysis of the issue with immediate implementation and feedback. They could be assigned to design a product's or service's development and launch, to move it into commercially viable production or service delivery, to ensure good maintenance, or to ensure effective after-sales service, or to guaranteeing 'future-proofing' where appropriate, and being open about product or service phase-out and replacement. It is then up to directors and managers to encourage an emotional climate which will switch the vast majority of their people into beginning to understand, and finally accepting, the necessity of such changes.

In explaining and measuring organizational adaptiveness we have been helped greatly by some of the staff of one of our clients, a financial services company in the UK's West Country. We were working on a large organizational transformation project, and after doing the Organizational Capability benchmarking, gap analysis identified four key issues which needed to be resolved in order to avoid organizational collapse. We used four action-learning groups, comprising six volunteers, each drawn from a cross section of senior to junior levels from departments throughout the organization. Each action-learning group had a top team member of the wider organization as its client. The client had ultimate line responsibility for the successful delivery of the project. The groups set off with great enthusiasm and, to their credit, all delivered a high quality and effectively implemented project in their nominated area, within the time-frame.

However, they also delivered a bonus – through their learning they developed a classification of the four main types of people's response to change which they had encountered as they tried to analyse, synthesize, implement and learn from their projects. In their model they designed two axes: understanding the issue; and the energy needed to tackle the necessary changes. Within these they created a quadrant:

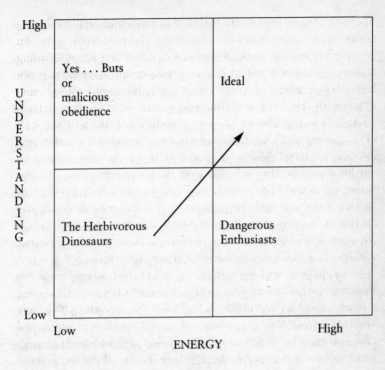

Figure 17 People's reaction to change

The 'Herbivorous Dinosaurs' had a low understanding of the issues and what was trying to be achieved, combined with low energy levels. In this particular organization there were many of these, as it had been coasting for over five years under very *laissez-faire* management and with little directoral pressure. People in this group did not want to know of any proposed changes and, provided they were paid, were happy to direct their main energies outside the company – for example in running community groups and sailing clubs. They were seen by their colleagues as slow and ponderous although they did, just, an adequate job. As one of the project managers commented: 'They are like herbivorous dinosaurs – their brain is so small that if they were being eaten from the tail by a raptor they would be half digested before their nervous system told them that they were in trouble.' Many organizations seem to have a significant number of such dinosaurs.

The 'Dangerous Enthusiasts' were a small and excitable group who undoubtedly had high energy levels, but sadly little understanding of what was intended, or the subtleties of getting there. They tended to be deeply frustrated by the existing organizational structure and processes, and had complained about them many times in the past. So, when presented with the chance of organizational change, they leapt at it. Unfortunately, they seemed less inclined to listen and to understand the purpose, vision and values contexts in which the change was designed to happen. They were high on the very idea of change. They rushed about the organization as unofficial, uncontrollable, apostles of the directors and managers, randomly walking into their own, and others', work groups to pass on wrong or twisted messages, haranguing others, urging them to change quicker, and usually creating reciprocal anger in return – a form of organizational Brownian Motion over which managers and directors had little direct control. They were useful in small doses as a way of unsettling the old inertia, but because they rarely linked into the formal organizational structure and processes they were, despite their rhetorical claims, mainly a hindrance to creating sustainable organizational adaptiveness. They were the shadow side of the informal organization, and risked giving e-motions a bad name again.

The Yes . . . Buts or 'Malicious Obedience' brigade comprised a large number of street-smart and well-educated people who did not want to confront change in their essentially comfortable, if rather boring and mildly frustrating, working life. They were intelligent enough to understand immediately what was required of them, but had none of the e-motional energy to want to do much about it. This drove the Dangerous Enthusiasts mad.

The 'Yes . . . Buts' were able to agree easily with any proposal in rational terms. However, their 'yes' was followed quickly by an entirely rational 'but', and then by reasons for doing nothing, at least for the moment. Emotionally this was reassuring for them, as they had been seen to agree with the top team, and had then been helpful in explaining why it could not be done now. They would have felt quite disconcerted if they had come out with a direct 'no', yet that was clearly their meaning. Many directors and managers fail to grasp that a 'yes . . . but' is a 'no', and so create a much less adaptive organization than the one they expected, based on their staff's words. 'Yes . . . Buts' are the modern equivalent of the phrase used by the aide to the megalomaniacal Lord Copper in Evelyn Waugh's *Scoop*. Even when his employer was telling the most outrageous lies and asking for confirmation that he was right, the aide could never say an outright 'no'. His response was always the wimpish 'up to a point Lord Copper'.

If directors and managers insisted on pushing change through, after such a response, they were frequently surprised when a superficially rational, but intensely emotionally negative, campaign was launched against them. This would not be a direct assault, but involved calculated use of 'malicious obedience' on a large scale. Participants in the campaign would start by saying 'Well, I have warned you of the consequences, but if you insist on pushing the changes through then we will, of course, obey your orders.' This is done explicitly, even over-explicitly. They would do no more, and no less, than they were told. However, if the managerial instructions were not sufficiently precise (and few are, because they assume a level of trust and the application of common sense by the receiver), they would carry out the instruction regardless of the consequences, even if they knew this would harm the organization.

When challenged they would utter the famous cop-out: 'We were only obeying orders.' Strictly, this was true, but it poisoned the emotional climate for long periods. This group was the most difficult for the directors and managers to align and attune, but it was essential that they did so, as they did not want to have a permanent and disloyal opposition in place.

The 'Ideals' quadrant did not exist but were a useful aspiration. It was our job to help directors and project managers align and attune the three 'difficult' groupings so that they participated in the urgent resolution of the four key issues. This was done through the pilot action-learning projects, and later transfer-of-learning projects, using existing staff rather than outside consultants. The success of these, essentially self-help, groups reinforced the energies of those staff who were moving towards the changes, and so began to reduce the power of those with little, and negative, energy. Within eighteen months the effects were extraordinary. A dedicated team of some 100, initially sceptical, people working in shifts twenty-four hours a day for a year on the major transformation project – redesign and implementation of the total central processing activities of the organization – not only delivered to time, to quality and within budget, but also won a world prize for the best example of such a transformational project. Even the Yes ... Buts had to admit that this switched the emotional temperature from negative to positive.

If more than eighty per cent of your organization is roughly aligned and attuned with your aspirations towards change then you are doing very well. If you have ninety per cent then you are doing very well indeed. If you have one hundred per cent, then you are deluding yourself. Human organizations are never like that.

Adaptiveness to change relies on trust, goodwill, intelligence, self-interest, understanding, common sense and, most of all, conscious critical review and learning within and between work groups. Increasing these values and processes of adaptiveness in daily working life is a major challenge for directors and managers.

10. CUSTOMER ORIENTATION

Given the importance of the 'moments of truth' already described, this needs to be the central focus for all the operational elements of Organizational Capability. Without it no one gets paid. Except in some extreme authoritarian regimes, organizations do not exist for their own benefit, and we sometimes need reminding of this. The cardinal sin in any enterprise is to lose touch with the customer base – even long-standing, major corporations do this. In the last decade such giants as IBM, Apple Computers, Coca-Cola, Marks and Spencers, General Motors and McDonalds, in their home market, did precisely that. Losing contact with the customer can happen easily, and the consequences can escalate rapidly and alarmingly. Coke is a good example: a new team, interestingly without a US citizen in the top three, decided that it was time to launch New Coke. Warning bells did not ring to say that the total replacement of such a US icon might be unwise, so the product was launched, and despite global hype, the consequences were both unwanted and came quickly. A hurried damage limitation exercise was launched to revive what is now Classic Coke, while running Diet Coke in parallel, and some form of calm was restored. There were red faces for the top team, but they had the honesty to admit that they had learned powerful lessons about the emotional power of brands, and the risk of upsetting a devoted fan's perception of equity. Both Cokes are now doing well.

This example also reinforces the maxim that 'only customers buy products, a market never bought anything'. Indeed Adam Smith's 'invisible hand' of the markets? was seen by him not only as the aggregation of individual choices, but also (Smith being a moral philosopher rather than an economist) an ethical force for good. Both elements can easily be forgotten by marketing departments dealing at the strategic level, but sales people and customer-facing staff know better. They should be the major source of information back to managers and directors of changing customer demand. The Organizational Capability issue is to ensure that such feedback and debating systems are properly geared to customer-orientation, rather than reinforcement of the organization's self-fulfilling stereotypes about their customers.

Customer-facing staff in such departments as telephone answering, telephone selling, service centres, support and maintenance and sales can have a major impact on raising the quantity and quality of customer feedback. They can also destroy a brand if they are forced to repeat the party line on all customer comments and complaints. When customer feedback is reinforced by regular and rigorous gap analysis by independent surveyors this is an invaluable source of discerning customer preferences and changing needs. Like data on competitor orientation, gap analysis needs to be focused centrally and be available on an intranet so that it then can be linked with open and constructive critical review and continuing organizational dialogue.

Gap analysis can be a cost-effective mechanism for greatly increasing Organizational Capability. If it also increases the volume of repeat sales this has a doubly beneficial effect, as it reduces the cost-of-sales, and those repeat customers will usually be willing to pay a small price premium, thereby improving profitability. This is the type of message that directors and managers can transmit throughout the organization to make a significant impact on overall profitability in the short and medium term.

Meta-elements of the Organizational Capabilities Model

11. LEADERSHIP ORIENTATION

All organizations are held together by the quantity and quality of their leadership and their learning climate.

The directors have a distinct job to do. The Latin root of their job title means 'to show the way ahead, and to give leadership'. To do this they must handle continuously their perennial dilemma of driving the enterprise forwards, while keeping it under prudent control. They can delegate much of this to managers, supervisors and staff, but will always retain ultimate accountability for it under the law. They are the direction-givers, the leaders of the total organization. In the military there is a classic axiom: 'The acid test of whether you are a good leader is whether you have any followers.' It is a salutary experience to be given the title of a leader and to rush ahead into the brave new world of organizational change, only to find that there is no one following you. The 'Dinosaurs' and 'Yes . . . Buts' will watch with mild interest while the 'Dangerous Enthusiasts' will run off in all directions.

Being a leader is about having the competences to blend the 'hard' task elements of work with the 'soft' social-process elements to achieve goals and purpose. This means developing the personal sensitivity, and the personal capacity, to have a portfolio of leadership styles which can be matched appropriately to the work in hand. Appropriateness depends on the maturity of the work group concerned. Maturity can be described on two axes. First, the orientation of the work group's members towards the task itself – are they new, with little experience of doing this work – or at the other end of the axis – are they a very mature group who know precisely what they are doing and will call on their leader for guidance only in times of great uncertainty? Second, their orientation towards each other – how inducted, included and competent are the members of the group? Are they all new and very unused to working together, or are they well-integrated and effectively self-managing? Combining the two axes allows one to see a range of four leadership styles which are appropriate for groups of different maturities.

It is important that the leader, whether of a work group or of the whole organization, has sufficient behavioural flexibility to cope with the very different demands of the various stages of the maturity cycle. Using a small group as an example, a leader faced with a new group is wise to assume, until proved otherwise, that they know little and are raw at working together. This means that

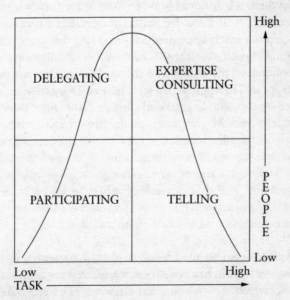

Figure 18 **Appropriate leadership styles during the development of a work group**

the leader will need to spend a significant amount of time telling them what to do and showing them how to do it. The leader needs to keep a close focus on first getting the work done, while beginning to build the group's internal relationships so that its members start to learn how to work together. The appropriate leadership style at this stage is 'Telling'.

As time progresses, the leader can relax a little on the task side, if the group is accepting some delegated power and producing sufficient volume and quality of work. The leader can then start to develop the group's personal relationships further. This progresses over time to an 'Expertise', style of leadership, where the group increasingly takes over more of the task leadership but still needs 'selling' the practice of learning to work together.

After that the going gets tougher, especially for the many leaders who are locked into the belief that their job is all about 'command-and-obey' structures. Real learning comes when the leader sufficiently trusts both the work quality and the relationships of the work group to begin to ease off the focus on both task and people. This is not a dereliction of duty, but a necessary stage in the group's maturation process – avoiding this stage will block the group's ability to learn. Task and social cohesion power is being offered to the group, and the leader is testing whether they can accept it. The appropriate style here is 'Delegating'.

Once the group has passed through the first three stages successfully then it can move, under supervision, into 'Participating'. The leader intervenes only by exception, as the group effectively becomes fully self-managing. The word 'participation' comes from the Latin root meaning joint ownership and joint responsibility, and that is precisely what the leader is seeking at this final stage of group maturity. However, the leader will still be fully accountable for the work group's actions.

An immediate problem with this progression towards maturity is that leaders tend to have one or two preferred personal leadership styles to which they become habituated. They need coaching to widen their personal portfolio of leadership styles so that they can embrace all four. Leaders with only one approach to leadership are usually unadaptive, and are often positively dangerous in a fast-changing world.

This can sound strange to leaders whose preferences are either firmly on the right or the left side of the leadership model. For the right-siders the problem is usually in getting them to let go sufficiently so that the group can begin to self-manage its normal routines, while accepting that they still need leadership. For left-siders who like groups to get on and manage themselves it can be intensely frustrating to be faced with a new group who initially need a lot of telling and expert advice. Left-siders are often bored and frustrated by the right-side processes, and so tend to rush them, only to find that the group rarely self-manages well, because there have not been sufficient induction, inclusion and competence-building processes. Such groups may achieve the tasks set, but they can fly apart very easily because they do not have the emotional resilience to cope with problems.

Taking a work group from Telling to Participation is a definition and a measure of an effective leadership style. It requires a leader to be able to learn, but once achieved it can be applied at any level in the organization. Directors often unwittingly follow the same processes when they carve out time to do their real work of policy formulation/foresight and strategic thinking. They have to give up some or all of their previous managerial, or professional, work to concentrate on direction-giving, and let go of the habitual comfort of their managerial, or professional, career to learn effective policy practices and strategic thinking. This is often a particularly difficult period for them, because they have invested so many years in becoming expert in their previous role. It is the board chairman's job to take a director to such competence.

12. LEARNING CLIMATE

It is not worth embarking on an analysis of Organizational Capability unless the directors, and the emotional climate, encourage the total organizational learning process of:

- Data collection
- Critical review of gap analysis
- Open debate of the issues
- Priority setting for remedial action
- Risk Assessment
- Pilot action-learning projects
- Guaranteed implementation of the results.
- Continuous learning processes

Many new managing directors try to make a lot of changes soon after coming into the post. They are frequently derailed by their managers and staff over the next year as the Yes . . . Buts get the upper hand. After the MD's initial round of downsizing, informal alliances of Dinosaurs, Yes . . . Buts and Dangerous Enthusiasts get to work, to stop or divert forward movement. This is usually reinforced by an organizational culture which accepts as normal the hiding of mistakes, blaming others, keeping one's head down and generally failing to learn. Over time such an organization is faced with corporate amnesia – no one can remember why things are done in certain ways. They just are.

This negative learning climate can develop into a more advanced form of not just making mistakes and blaming others but of covering up, and in its highest form, of then covering up the cover-ups. The amount of organizational time, money and sheer physical and mental energy needed to maintain this negative climate is colossal. Some report that blaming and hiding costs four times as much as an open, critically reviewing and learning climate. The implications from the productivity point of view alone are profound for both directors and managers. If they can reduce the manufacturing process, service delivery and overhead costs by up to seventy-five per cent through developing a system which strives openly to 'get it right first time' and learn continuously from this, then their contribution to the overall health and development of the organization is enormous.

The operational systems which generate the organization's learning climate are the responsibilities of the line managers. The emotional climate for learning starts, however, with the directors' purpose, vision and values, and makes itself manifest by whether their behaviour is in line with the espoused values. The systems of learning must combine both the cycles of learning about the changing outside world (improving organizational effectiveness), and the cycles of learning about the internal operational world (improving organizational efficiency).

Ideally, we are seeking an organization where the two cycles combine and ensure continuous critical review to ensure that its rate of learning is equal to, or greater than, the rate of change in its environment:

$$L \geq C$$

to use Revans' famous axiom.

It takes both understanding and emotional energy from directors and managers to build systems and climate of constructive critical review and learning. While most can understand rationally the need for such learning, they rarely have the energy to do much about it. Many directors fall firmly into the Dinosaur, or Yes . . . But, category, despite the fact that it is their job to direct organizational change. This is why most learning comes at times of organizational crisis. Only when an organization is in deep trouble (for example, its main customer has just gone bust, or it has run out of budget for the year), or when there is massive change (it is being privatized, or taken over), do directors spring into action, and are often pleasantly surprised as to just how aligned and attuned most of the staff can be. Learning fast and well is in everybody's interest. They can then build on the values of accountability, openness and probity, to ask discriminating questions, to learn how to co-operate, and to generate excellence and trust in the organization and its customers or consumers.

APPLYING THE TWELVE ELEMENTS OF ORGANIZATIONAL CAPABILITY

When analysing and applying the twelve elements of Organizational Capability it must be remembered that:

- They are all integrated facets of the total organization.
- They must, therefore, overlap to some extent to bring different light and perspective to organizational issues.
- They are all measurable quantitatively and qualitatively using gap analysis.
- These gap analyses form the basis for informed choice and decisions.
- Unless the process is linked to systems of continuous organizational learning it is not worth starting to implement it.

Just how capable is your organization?

CHAPTER · 7

The Integration of Organizations

As the world grows more complex we need models and mind-sets which allow everyone in an organization to understand better their place in the total flow of work through the organization, and their role in learning to do this work more effectively and efficiently.

Consider the ideas behind the design of the learning organization:

- The double loop of learning connecting the external and internal worlds of the organization;
- The business brain processing the learning from the double loop and forming the forum of continuing dialogue and debate within the organization;
- The process of continuous critical review to inform that debate;
- and the emotional climate to encourage such learning and debate

This gives both a morally sound and pragmatic approach to achieving Organizational Capability.

Over the last decade it has been noticeable that such ideas are evolving into more integrated, holistic and measurable models of organization. These models explicitly attempt to integrate the many simultaneous processes of the organization. I have already referred to my initial work in *The Learning Organization* (see p. 62) and must acknowledge Peter Senge's later work *The Fifth Discipline*[32] which adds a distinctive systems thinking dimension.

To these I should add three models, described briefly below, which are in the process of evolution, and which seem worthy of further development.

THE SERVICE PROFIT CHAIN

This model came to my notice in a letter in the *Harvard Business Review*.[33] It interested me greatly because of its clear causal link between the retention of good customers and the retention of good staff, thus making a clear business case for what many had guessed intuitively.

Reading the model in reverse order from right to left, its argument states that the continuity of profit flow for an organization (or surplus for a non-profit) is dependent on customer retention. This may seem so prosaic as to be blindingly obvious, yet a surprising number of organizations are fuzzy about who their customers are, and what their changing needs are, and so are even fuzzier about how they can retain them. Economically speaking, a retained 'good' customer adds more value than a new customer because the costs of getting a new one are usually so much higher.

Good customers can be retained by maintaining their *perception* of external service or product quality. This perception is governed by the combination of 'hard' facts and 'soft' emotions surrounding the product which are then tested in relation to price. Brands are a good example of this perceptual combination of the forces of economic rationality and emotionality coming into play. Economic rationality says that it is good housekeeping to buy a store's own brand products which promise similar quality and characteristics to branded products, but at a lower price. Yet by advertizing and careful market segmentation we often form an emotional attachment to a particular branded product or service for which we will pay a price premium. We are convinced that this is good value for money unless we are very short of cash. Even then, if we buy the cheaper own brand, we feel that we are missing an often little understood 'something' from the branded item.

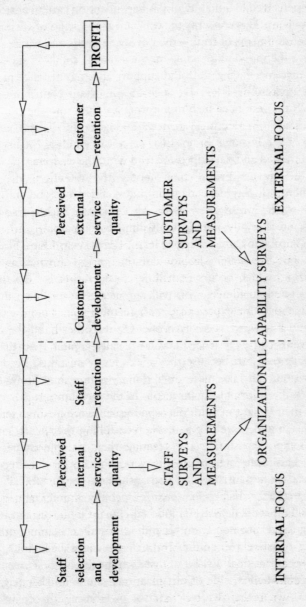

Figure 19 The service profit chain

The perceived external quality is dependent on careful customer development. This concerns the constant monitoring of customers and their moments of truth – their evolving needs and wants. This is where the marketing people on the strategic thinking side, and sales, customer-facing staff and support and maintenance people on the operations side, have such an important contribution to make. If the results of such monitoring are built into the continuing organizational critical review, dialogue and debate in the forum of the business brain, then perceived external quality can be maintained and developed for, and with, the customer.

In the service profit chain model the retention of good customers is highly dependent on the retention of good staff. By 'good' staff I mean those who are competent, interpersonally skilled, emotionally intelligent, willing to empathize with customers' problems and willing to learn. Given what I have already said about the current fashion for thoughtless downsizing and rightsizing, which occurs with little consideration for the retention of good customers, you will appreciate the problem. In an annual budget an experienced staff member looks more expensive than a new, inexperienced one. On the other hand the cost-effectiveness of experienced staff is usually greater than that of inexperienced staff because they make fewer mistakes, need less supervision, can take more discretionary action, and know how to work the informal organization. In the medium term they are worth their weight in gold. But who measures the medium term?

So more and more companies are deskilling their staff, giving them temporary status, and treating them as interchangeable units. This approach often sits very uneasily with directors' espoused values surrounding such issues as 'product excellence' and 'customer satisfaction'. Treating people as units of production will create a negative emotional climate in an organization, driving them into non-learning, hiding mistakes, blaming others, seeking negative recognition through malicious behaviour, and other organizational ills. All of these will be felt by the customers. This is the shadow side of organizational life and it is portrayed wonderfully in the cartoon character of Homer Simpson in *The Simpsons*. Homer is in a deskilled job – worryingly, a quality controller at his local nuclear power plant. His plans to cheat the system, particularly the evil owner Monty Burns, in order to sleep or eat all day rather than watch the controls, and his crazy examples of industrial indiscipline, are very funny, but ultimately chilling, if we take this as an example of the logical extension of deskilling to absurdity.

So why do organizations do it? Presumably because many directors and managers hold a simplistic notion that there is a golden mean to which all headcounts can be cut without affecting customer retention. This may be true in some economist's model but it is not true if people's emotions, both customers' and staffs', are added to the equation. Economics is known as 'the dismal science' with good reason. It tends to value 'economic rationalism' above all, because it cannot deal with emotions in its equations. It should be remembered that Adam Smith was not an economist but a philosopher concerned with 'moral sentiment'. We need better research into the rational and emotional trade-offs between the retention of good customers and the retention of good staff before we can have some resolution. The service profit chain gives some pointers here.

But the retention of experienced staff is not just about fighting the bottom-line fixation of managers. The model argues that equal importance should be given to the staff's perception of their organization's internal service quality. This reflects the idea that the flow of work through an organization leads to the production of a product or service which creates a sequence of interlocking internal customers or consumers. This is still a relatively new idea. The Total Quality Management movement has had a lot to do with developing this concept and giving it a statistical base, credibility and growing acceptance. It measures productivity throughout the workflow, identifies bottlenecks and blockages, and takes action to unblock them. Again, the importance of rigorous and regular ensuring of the quantity and quality of workflow, and staff satisfaction, is a key link in creating internal service quality standards. The subsequent learning is crucial for both organizational effectiveness and organizational efficiency.

From such data a system can be created which will upgrade

directors' and managers' focus on, and quality of, staff selection, training, competence building, and, ultimately, personal development for continuing employability, whether inside or outside the organization.

The service profit chain is a useful focus from which managers can begin to appreciate the relationships between the achievement of 'hard' tasks and 'soft' processes, through the measurement of improved profitability via regular critical review to ensure the retention of both good customers and good staff.

The EFQM Model for Business Excellence

The ideas of the service profit chain can be taken further. The model which has done so and is proving very useful and popular is the European Foundation for Quality Management's (EFQM) Business Excellence model.

In the last six years it has been used to benchmark effectively organizations in the private and public sectors and professional practices, in many countries across the European Union and beyond. The model strives to generate business excellence through carefully benchmarked, self-referenced 'enablers' (inputs):

- Leadership
- People management
- Policy and strategy
- Resources
- Processes

The total of these enablers generates fifty per cent of the total scoring on the model.

The 'results' (outputs) side consists of:

- People satisfaction
- Customer satisfaction
- Impact on society
- Business results

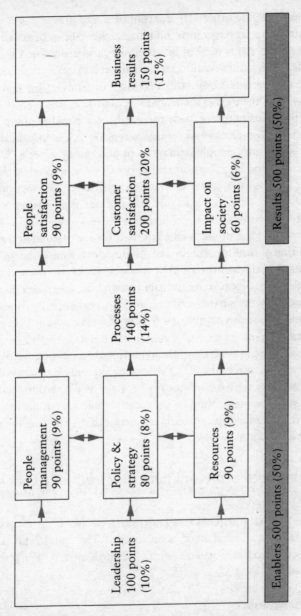

Figure 20 The EFQM model for business excellence

These provide the other fifty per cent of the scoring.

I do not intend to go into the internal weighting, or scoring, of the model here but further information can be obtained through EFQM.[34] What I do wish to stress is the reflection in the model of the theme of this book: the necessity of integrating task and process to achieve Organizational Capability.

On the enabler (input) side the need for a blend of 'hard' task and 'soft' social-emotional processes is accepted, seen particularly in the leadership, people management and policy aspects. On the results side the social-emotional processes are strongly reflected in the aspects of people satisfaction, customer satisfaction and impact on society. This is not the normal type of rationalist, managerial model.

The sum of the inputs and outputs is finally calculated through the business results. If a board of directors aspires to being a learning board, then the EFQM model is an excellent, and quantifiable, start to regularly and rigorously benchmarking, measuring progress, ensuring critical review, enhancing continuing dialogue about the organization's capabilities, taking action and learning from it.

By blending rationality and emotional processes across the whole organization the EFQM model expands on many of the issues addressed by the service profit chain, while setting them in a wider social context. 'Impact on society' makes an appearance for the first time in a popular business model that I am aware – a sign of things to come.

The Balanced Scorecard (and the Death of Annual Budgets)

An alternative integrative model that has also been growing in popularity is the balanced scorecared.[35] This model takes four perspectives on the organization's performance, and orientation towards:

- Shareholders
- Customers

- Internal operations
- Learning and innovation

It looks at the strategic intentions of the organization, and identifies key measures and targets in each of the four areas. It gets the directors and managers to specify where the organization needs to be on each of the four perspectives within a given timeframe to achieve their strategic intent. Then it benchmarks the current position on all four perspectives, does a gap analysis, and starts to bring into being action plans, resource allocations, milestones and budgets to bridge those gaps.

These performance gaps are addressed in detail by the managers and staff in terms of group and individual budget-setting, the integration of business plans, the allocation of capital resources, and, especially, the regular processes of feedback to achieve both innovation and learning. The inclusion of the latter is another breakthrough in conventional business models.

Such an approach seems to have two noticeable effects on Organizational Capability. At the policy and strategic thinking levels it helps to guide board directors' and senior managers' thinking and behaviour (and so staff commitment) away from a narrow focus on profitability or the return-on-capital figures. By consciously keeping the notion of balance, or trade-off, between the four key perspectives, it allows better critical review of an organization's market capitalization, i.e. what is its share of the new wealth created in its industry over the past years? The model helps give a much richer meaning to the increasingly popular mantra of 'creating shareholder value'. In addition, it has the huge benefit of stopping much of the organization's micro-political accounting games by benchmarking it against specific competitors, and final results are assessed by the financial markets. This is valuable, if sometimes uncomfortable, data at the strategic and board level. It is even more valuable for the shareholders.

At the operational level the balanced scorecard model has the huge advantage of putting the over-arching tyranny, even demonology, of the annual budget into its proper perspective. This

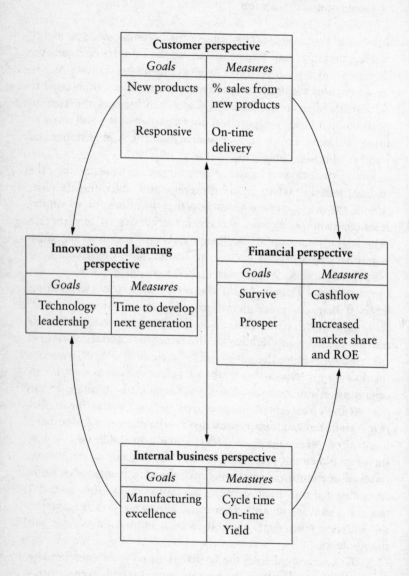

Figure 21 The balanced scorecard

constant source of irritation is a major block to releasing Organizational Capability.

It has always struck me as peculiar that otherwise sensible directors and managers, who have a passionate vision for the future, and who take imaginative decisions as to how to get there, habitually give much of their power to the finance department, due to an unswerving belief in the sanctity of the annual budget. There is no law that says performance reviews can only occur annually – only Annual General Meetings have to. Given the turbulent nature of an organization's external environment, it is greatly puzzling that the budgets are considered binding for a year, and that so much organizational time is devoted to them. Claiming that annual budgets have a mystique and power which transcend the organization's learning systems, and the importance of monitoring and adjusting regular business ratios and trendlines, is plain daft. Yet many organizations' behaviour is to believe just this and to stick to it unswervingly. Organizations need to be frequently rebalanced – hence the balanced scorecard concept.

What is going on? A 1996 survey of 400 US corporations showed that ninety-seven per cent used annual budgets to control corporate performance. No one declared that accountants are the only people deemed to have credible measures for organizational performance, indeed, James Thurber once described accountants as 'having no bowels', which could help to explain much of the strange, retentive behaviour that I see from some of them.

The twelve-month budget is one of the biggest blocks to releasing Organizational Capability at the operational level that I encounter. By keeping power in the hands of the finance department it allows the avoidance of 'soft' data which is much more important than financial figures in analysing present and future customer behaviour. 'Hard' data can always be rationalized. It is used as a prop by managers fearful of letting go of their budgetary power because they fear the consequences of having to cope with the growing, and unknown, turbulence in the outside world.

Two Swedish examples show that refusing to budget annually does not automatically cast you into anarchy and eternal corporate damnation. Svenska Handelsbanken, the leading Swedish bank, has moved away from traditional budgetary control and is making a cultural shift towards a focus on continuous improvement. It is attempting to organize itself so that people matter, using a process which balances control with people's e-motional energies and learning, and with the drive towards the organization's strategic intent. For a bank this is a remarkable transformation.

As early as 1970 it dropped annual accounting when it set out to consciously outperform the industry average each year. It has done this consistently since 1972 to become Sweden's largest bank. Instead of top-down budgetary control the directors have encouraged a culture which combines thrift with continuous improvement. Each branch acts as an independent business unit and has transparent communications, so that it can share its performance, and its consequent learning, with all the other branches. The results are impressive. The cost/income ratio has been reduced to forty-five per cent compared with seventy per cent for its main international rivals, while return on equity averages twenty per cent, which has certainly kept the shareholders happy.

ABB, the Swedish-Swiss multinational specializing in heavy electrical engineering, heavy transportation systems and information technology, has taken a similar route under the dynamic Percy Barnevik. He flattened the organizational pyramid, drastically reduced head office staff and their control powers, and created a set of moral values and behaviours throughout the corporation. This is where his previously mentioned concept of federations comes in. Independent, smallish units of around two to three hundred people each were created throughout the organization, usually below the 'strategic business unit' size, so that they frequently had to negotiate with each other and contract together to win large international projects. The culture of ABB was defined in a policy statement which is a very long way away from the usual fixation on the bottom line: 'members will interact with mutual confidence, respect, and trust . . . to eliminate the we/they attitude . . . and to remain flexible, open and generous'. This sets a constructive climate for the development of the balanced scorecard approach. The statement also sets an emotional climate which encourages the creation of strong, open, inter-personal networks across the organization, and rewards innovation and learning.

Organizational Integration

Much of the strategy surrounding the organizational integration found in such companies as Svenska Handelsbanken, ABB, Hewlett Packard and Unipart is distilled by Christopher Bartlett and Sumantra Ghoshal in their book *Beyond the M-form: Towards a Managerial Theory of the Firm*.[36] 'M-form' refers here to the traditional multi-divisional structure of corporations. As the turbulence of markets increases so does the need to be closer to the customers and staff, and to this they add comments on the radical impact of information management systems. Bartlett and Ghoshal argue that they can identify three core, integrative processes for organizations of the future:

- The entrepreneurial process in which the front-line operators are nearer to the key strategists and decision-takers, constantly seeking out new business opportunities.
- The integration process by which middle management convey information across the organization, as well as between themselves and external partners.
- The renewal process by which the directors and senior managers give inspiration and a sense of purpose through leadership, frequently challenging the status quo.

I feel their analysis chimes well with the theme of this book. If we are to create capable organizations for the twenty-first-century then we have to take the idea of the organization as an integrated, inter-connected, living system much more seriously. After all, that is what the word originally meant.

CHAPTER 8

Power Shifts Shaping the Twenty-first-Century Organization

Will Organizational Capabilities change as we enter the twenty-first-century? To try and answer this question it is wise to set out the few facts we have, and to attempt to deduce trends from them.

The external environments of all organizations are being re-shaped as the limits to the easy acceptance of the idea of 'global capitalism' are being reached. As I write, gloomy reports from all around the world of 'economic melt-down' in Japan, Russia, South-east Asia and South America are on most newscasts. Dire predictions are being made that the US and Europe could be dragged into another Great Depression, and the possibilities of rampant nationalism, even war, are being aired all too freely.

Behind much of this uncertainty lie distinct patterns, most of which are driven as much by emotion as by any form of economic rationality. Economically, the roots of the immediate global economic problems can be traced back directly to the devaluation of the Chinese yuan in 1994. This set off competitive devaluations in the South-east Asian currencies which finally flagged up warning signals for global investors that they were pouring money into increasingly volatile economies. This began to stir their emotions as well as their logic, although most investors rapidly went into denial, and chose to ignore the signals of deterioration until matters became much more dangerous. As inward investor nervousness increased, little was done by the Japanese, Russian, South-east Asian, Chinese or Brazilian governments to create reassurance. Indeed, many went ahead with even grander plans for property development, new infrastructures and more manufacturing facilities.

It needs be remembered that the present crisis was triggered by the foreign exchange crisis in Thailand. This was an essentially emotional issue about trust in a government's ability to keep its economy, and hence its foreign exchange rates, under control. Increasingly, inward investors did not trust the Thai government's plan or controls. Then, the foreign exchange speculators moved in on what looked more and more like a one-way bet. It was. This led to general investor concern, and later panic, around the region about rampant 'crony capitalism' in Indonesia, the Philippines, Malaysia and China, where even the Communist Party has started to take action over the abuse of party power positions to line personal, family and friends' pockets.

As the investors' blinkers lifted, the sudden distrust and fear (very powerful emotions) of most of the Asian Tiger economies became manifest. In Japan, formerly the second largest driver of the world economy, matters were made worse by blatant abuse of political power, particularly through the acceptance of bribes both by the governing party, and the previously much heralded epitome of integrity and national wealth creation – the Ministry of Finance.[37]

The situation then declined even further due to the well-publicized weakness of Boris Yeltsin's presidency and the consequent rise and rise of 'gangster capitalism' in Russia. Here, powerful new bankers and industrialists took a similar robust, and, occasionally, extra-legal approach to capturing monopoly markets, as their US counterparts had done over a hundred years before. Similar doubts are being raised about Brazil, the rest of South America, and now even the Mediterranean economies of Europe after the faltering launch of the euro.

Most of this investor uncertainty was not based on the economic fundamentals of these countries, but on the quality of national and corporate governance – the systems, processes and values by which governments and corporations are directed. Corporate governance relies totally on the underlying emotional and ethical issues of accountability, trust, probity and transparency amongst directors and owners. Whereas for some centuries, accepted levels of corruption in the countries mentioned above (and many others) were seen merely as the local way of doing business, the instantaneous speed of communication around the globe, coupled with the fast-growing need for inward investors to have much more robust, transparent and reliable banking, financial and civil law systems, means that the spotlight is coming to bear on the national and corporate governance systems of such countries.

These systems are proving grossly inadequate, and rather panicky reguests for instant international solutions to deep systemic and cultural problems are being made. This cannot happen in the short term, despite the unrealistic demands made on the OECD, IMF, World Bank and G7, but the consequences of such increasingly global demands will have a major effect on the design of our national and corporate organizations, both private and public. We are going to have to face a major rethinking of the purpose and nature of our organizations as social institutions if we are to cope. What this means for their Organizational Capabilities is open to debate.

CHANGING ORGANIZATIONS

To return to the level of organizations after such a global *tour de horizon* may seem rather prosaic, but I think that some of this rethinking is already occurring at international, national and corporate levels. In some ways the corporates, private and public, may well be providing the pilot action-learning schemes which will signal larger societal, enterprise and cultural changes.

As we can see from the Svenska Handelsbanken and ABB examples in the previous chapter, from the design of BA's new Waterside headquarters building, which is laid out like a village street to break the old BA habits and militaristic mindset, and from the culture changes at BMW-Rover, Jaguar and Unipart, where workers and self-managed work groups are being given greater flexibility in their work processes, radical approaches are being used to create more effective Organizational Capability for the new century. Major debates are occurring in many parts of the world, both in private and public sectors, about the possible shapes of post M-form organizations. The twentieth century's organizational gift to civilization was the modern bureaucracy – what will be the twenty-first-century equivalent?

Will we see organizations develop so that people and their emotions really matter? Will we see a conscious and continuous balancing of task achievement with effective social processes? I think that we will. There are at least three distinct forces at work to bring this about:

- Pressures on ownership and corporate responsibility
- Pressures of a moral and ethical nature on, and in, organizations
- Pressure to improving profitability through learning

Pressures on Ownership and Corporate Responsibility

The nature of the ownership of large corporations is changing. The growing global power of multinational corporations over the very sovereignty of nations in a global economy is causing concern, especially in those weak nations, where rich corporations can exercise undue influence. We are beginning to understand that for too long we have let limited liability companies effectively do what they wish. Bob Monks in his book *The Emperor's Nightingale: Restoring the Integrity of the Corporation* points out that Adam Smith queries in *The Wealth of Nations* (the very bible of modern capitalism) the creation of limited liability, joint stock companies with their own legal personality. He saw that this new corporate legal form was necessary to allow the rapid expansion of enterprise, but that it would also give companies:

- Unlimited size
- Unlimited life

- Unlimited licence
- Unlimited power

He predicted that this would eventually have a devastating effect on society and nations as the companies outgrew them. Interestingly, I found a similar concern in Abraham Lincoln's diary, dated 21 November 1864, as he contemplates the consequences for the nation after the end of the Civil War:

> We may congratulate ourselves that this cruel war is nearing its end. It has cost a vast amount of treasure and blood . . . It has indeed been a trying hour for the Republic; but I see in the near future a crisis approaching that unnerves me and causes me to tremble for the safety of my country. As a result of the war, corporations have been enthroned and an era of corruption in high places will follow, and the money power of the country will endeavour to prolong its reign by working upon the prejudices of the people until all wealth is aggregated in a few hands and the Republic is destroyed. I feel at this moment more anxiety for the safety of my country than ever before, even in the midst of war. God grant that my suspicions may prove groundless.

At a time when nearly fifty per cent of the world's richest organizations are now corporations rather than countries, one can appreciate his point. Whose values, purpose, visions and policies will they follow? Whose culture will be paramount? An immediate example is the concerned debate about the US's Monsanto Corporation, and its moves to dominate world crop and insecticide production through genetic engineering, or modification. This ignores many smaller governments' economic and environmental concerns, especially about the long-term effects on the eco-systems of the introduction of new plant types. Monsanto reassures us that all is well, but there are no long-term studies to confirm this. We simply do not know. People's negative emotions are triggered by their lack of trust in big business's propensity to do the right thing for stakeholders as well as shareholders.

Abraham Lincoln's concerns linger on. Additionally, repeated use of the adjective 'scientific' in press releases in an attempt to smother debate tends to raise hackles rather than reassure.

In the US, both government and corporations have a history of over-optimism in such areas. Corporate amnesia can be writ large, as the lessons from history are ignored. The settlement of the Badlands of Dakota and Montana is a classic example of the emotions of betterment and greed creating an 'emperor's clothes' syndrome. Hundreds and thousands of people wanted to enter into an apparently bountiful economic and emotional contract. Settlement of the region was encouraged by a combination of the US government and the new railway companies, banks, farm machinery manufacturers and city authorities across the US and Europe, who wanted to clear out their slums. A grand picture was painted of the 'free land' available, and the guaranteed future of anyone willing to work a half section (320 acres). Tens of thousands took up the offer and the loans, fenced off high plains prairie, planted, and found that their first years were indeed good. They were encouraged by the 'scientific' basis of Mr Campbell's Dry Agricultural Methods, and felt they had entered a truly Panglossian world where all was for the best in the best of all possible worlds. Warnings from the ranchers who knew the high plains well, about the fragility of the soil, (there was less than an inch of topsoil) and the perversity of the climate, went unheeded. After some damp years, in 1919 the climate returned to its usual hot and dry state, for which the homesteaders were unprepared. The earth baked, crops and cattle died, banks failed, and the dreams of thousands and thousands of people turned literally to dust. The early informal coalition fell apart and its disinformation and motives were bitterly criticized. The emotional contract with the settlers was well and truly broken as brilliantly described in Jonathan Raban's book *Bad land*.[38] When grand schemes are mentioned today, are matters that different? Cynics will say 'no'.

However, I can detect signs of a slow rethinking process in the air which will transform the nature of our organizations, particularly our businesses, as institutions. In the private sector this is coming mainly through the changing nature of the ownership of corporations, and in the active interest that these new owners take in organizations' performance and conformance. Two overlapping groups seem to be driving this forward: 'shareholder activists'; and 'pensioner power'. Looking at the figures for the market capitalization of pension funds across leading economies, the growing power of the pension funds and insurance companies alone is awesome.

Funds handling financial portfolios on behalf of their pensioner owners are now coming under critical, and more public, review much more frequently. This increasingly affects the corporations as well. 'Shareholder activists' demand much greater transparency of financial affairs and board processes.

Recent examples of the impact of shareholder activists can be seen in the publicly constructively critical behaviour of fund-managers such as CalPERS, Hermes/LENS, and PIRC (Pensions and Investments Research Consultants) towards major corporations in which they hold shares or bonds. Shareholder activists are especially concerned about financial performance and corporate governance issues such as board composition and board performance, but their interests now extend to such issues as problems of environmental pollution, worker health and safety issues and human rights abuses. They actively take up such issues with the respective boards at annual general meetings and extraordinary general meetings, collecting proxy votes for their cause. Through soliciting proxy votes from other shareholders who support their analyses of company performance, they are becoming a force to reckon with for chairmen and managing directors. Shareholder activists feel that they should not just buy and sell shares on the margin to register their approval or disapproval of a company's performance. They are in for the long haul, and will use critical review processes of board performance and conformance to stay there. Shareholder activists are very interested in the manifestations and measurement of Organizational Capability.

Pensioner power is part of the key to understanding this. Pension funds are held in trust by fund managers on behalf of the pension subscribers. Previously pensioners have been very passive, but a new generation of pensioners are now realizing their power

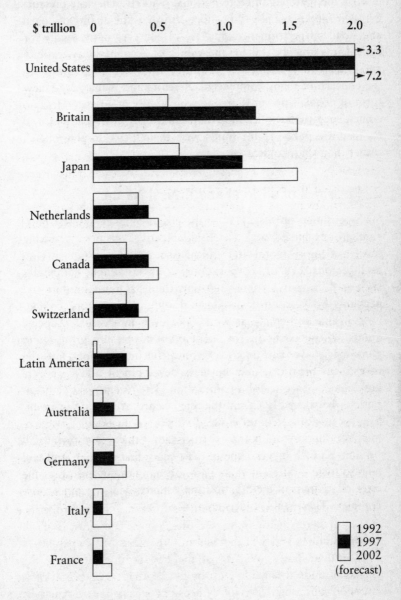

Figure 22 World pension assets

in both the national and international markets. They are pressuring their fund managers to be more critical of the quality of board and financial performance, and are calling ever more loudly for ethical investments and for the values of accountability, probity and transparency to be demonstrated by board behaviour – to the concern of many complacent directors and managers. A new form of people's power is arising which will not go away. It is no coincidence that the leading funds like CalPERS, Hermes and RailPen are public sector funds with their focus on pensioners', rather than shareholders', needs.

2. Pressures of a Moral and Ethical Nature

Such pensioner power, allied to the power of single-interest pressure groups linked with shareholder activist groups, is raising more and more moral and ethical issues about investments in, and performance of, corporations. It is noticeable companies such as BP and ICI publish not only the legal annual report and accounts but also an environmental audit, and in some companies, health and safety at work, and even intellectual property audits. Loose coalitions of single-interest pressure groups and pensioner power can make very powerful interventions into the investment practices, new business development and corporate governance processes of a corporation. The recent positive negotiations between PIRC and the Shell board are a case in point. The successful outcomes covered corporate governance, enviromental pollution and human rights issues. Ethical investment will become a much bigger issue in the twenty-first century, and will help to form a different value base for many organizations as the inter-relatedness of the organization's stakeholders becomes more complex. These stakeholders comprise:

- Shareholders
- Customers
- Staff
- Suppliers
- Legislators and regulators

- Impact on society
- Local communities

The *Tomorrow's Company* report of the Royal Society of Arts[39] makes very interesting reading in this area of corporate social responsibility. It also raises the interesting possibility that more democratic processes may come into being in private and public-sector organizations in the future. Democracy exists in a limp form in private organizations through the shareholders' power to vote at AGMs and EGMs. It is being extended at an operational level by the development of federal organizational structures, and by the reduction in the number of managers and the growth of self-managing work groups. How far will organizational democracy develop over the next decade? Will, for example, certain types of stakeholder be given any form of voting power? If we are serious about developing good corporate citizenship, the concept of democracy will have to be developed.

While these external pressures for reshaping power in organizations are growing, there are also many other internal forces working to create change. One is the issue of to whom boards and directors will be accountable in the twenty-first-century organization. The law in most countries is simple – the answer is to the owners, the shareholders. But as the stakeholder idea develops there will be increasing accountability, backed by legislation, to stakeholders, even though most of them do not directly own in the company. This will make life more complicated for directors and managers, but it will also be the beginning of the wider acceptance of the idea of the organization as a complex adaptive learning system.

Coupled with this increasing accountability is the legal concept, increasingly accepted in many countries, that all directors are equal in the boardroom. This challenges two long-held, cosy notions. First, that only the chairman and managing director have real directoral power, so that only they are accountable. Second, that there is a distinction between executive directors and non-executive directors. In most jurisdictions there is not. If the idea that all directors are equal is enforced through the rigorous application of the law, then we may well see better induction, inclusion and competence building in boards, which must have a positive effect on the acceptance and measurement of organizational competences. This, in turn, should make organizations much better places for everyone to work in.

In the UK the directoral values of accountability, probity and transparency are being taken further by the establishment of director accreditation and registration systems, for example the Institute of Directors' 'Chartered Director' status. It is possible that at some point the stock exchange, or government, may ask for compulsory accreditation and registration of new directors of publicly listed companies, and in the public sector. Directing will become a regulated profession in such organizations, which will hopefully help to end crony capitalism, hints of which are still found at the top of too many organizations.

It is certain that the rather fuzzy present thinking about appointing directors who are representatives of other parties will be brought to a head in many countries and then clarified in the next century. At present it is often assumed that groups such as shareholders, trades unions, community groups, pressure groups and governments can appoint, through the necessary process, people who will represent their values and views on a board and take decisions on their behalf. In many jurisdictions this is not so – once a person is appointed a director then their first priority is not to the group which they represent but to the company itself as a legal entity. It can be a salutary lesson if the interests and values they represent are in conflict with the needs of the company. As courts become tougher in enforcing the law that the primary duty of a director is to their company as a separate legal entity, it will be interesting to see the effect that this has on, for example, many of Continental Europe's 'two tier' boards, and on the idea of legislation for worker directors on boards. This should have a major effect on the Organizational Capabilities of leadership, and organizational clarity.

3. Pressure to Improving Profitability through Learning

The shareholder versus stakeholder argument is sterile. The essential trick is to learn how to combine the two. The major shifts in the powers within an organization required to do this will also emphasize the importance of a learning climate and personal and group Performance Indicators, which will have a positive effect on long-term survival and profitability.

In private companies, formal power will still be delegated by shareholders to the directors. How the directors deal with this power in order to increase profitability brings us back not just to a focus on cost-reduction, but to the cost-effectiveness of learning from all previous actions. This means breaking away from finance-dominated approaches, and instead combining a rational, figures-driven approach with the emotional commitment of a values-driven approach. A value is a belief in action.

To do this well it is necessary to design organizations which acknowledge and use the power of the informal organization. This involves changing the mindsets so that everybody is rewarded for seeking continuous improvement to the workflows and output quality, within an integrated organization. To do this many of the old concepts stemming from pyramidal structures must be rethought.

INFORMATION AND LEARNING

Tapping into the informal organization's social-emotional processes releases much new information into the organizational learning systems, which reduces the tendency of some, particularly middle managers, to hoard information and use selected amplification or attenuation of messages to retain the pivotal power. Critical review and debate meetings, whistle-blowers, action learning groups, e-mail, intranets, Internet and web sites (official and unofficial) release such a wealth of data into the organization that the ability to hoard information is greatly reduced, while the problem of selecting appropriate information is greatly increased. In the short term this can have a negative effect and lead to information overload, unless managed sensitively. People cannot easily read or listen to, let alone react to, large numbers of incoming messages. As they try to cope, their working day lengthens and tiredness, then ill health, sets in. The positive and negative benefits of information power will be a major feature of Organizational Capabilities in the future.

Learning to learn will become a meta-competence, so that people will be able to ask more discriminating questions of the veritable mountains of data.

INTER-WORK GROUP CONNECTIONS

The Handelsbanken and ABB examples (see pp. 155-6) are important because they build on the idea of generating and maintaining trust as a key lubricant between work groups. By openly sharing information they can get more effective critical reviews both within and between groups throughout the company more quickly, using the power of both the formal and informal organization. Their rate of learning is closer to the rate of external change. I think it worth repeating Percy Barnevik's policy and values statement on the creation of Organizational Capability at ABB: 'individuals will interact with mutual confidence, respect and trust to eliminate the we/they attitude . . . and to remain flexible, open and generous'. This is a very interesting values statement and one I would commend for any organization. In ABB this values-based code of behaviour governs both how staff are consciously encouraged to develop strong personal and operational networks, with a strong framework of values based on confidence, trust and respect.

These ideas reinforce the need for systems which enable continuing organizational dialogue. This dialogue is both internal, through the critical review mechanisms, and external, through contacts with the main stakeholders. In private organizations customer-facing staff need to strengthen their dialogue with the customers and their changing needs, operations and procurement staff need to get closer to their suppliers, directors need to be closer to the investors, legislators, local communities and customers. Everybody needs to think about protecting the physical environment and health and safety at work. The systems for learning how to carry out a continuous critique and develop organizational learning are the responsibility of the directors as they sit at the organization's central process – the 'business brain'.

These developmental learning processes are similar in public sector organizations. Here, moving the organizational culture to one of responsiveness and learning can be an even harder task than in a private company, but it can be done. Indeed, it has to be done, as in many countries the cost of government is penal and, as the cost of national or local government is directly related to personal and corporate taxation, in such a situation the country has little capacity to be enterprising. The more effective and efficient the governmental sector, the lower the taxes and so the higher the profitability of the private sector which, as it improves its volumes through lower costs, can pay even more taxes. This virtuous circle has rarely been achieved, except perhaps in Hong Kong.

Most countries still tend to adopt a more thoughtless, bottom-line approach, rigidly reinforced by annual budgets, and with no way of ensuring that cost-effectiveness is analysed properly. This can be done by looking at the wider system that public department serves, the sums invested in the competence of the staff employed, the experience base of the organization and then any proposed cuts. These are complicated calculations, but once the Organizational Capabilities measures are in place they can be made and accepted. This will not always please a minister who has the perspective of a one-year budget, but it is worth doing for the benefit of the social, as well as the economic, development of that country.

VALUING PEOPLE

As both private and public sectors move away from the mass employment of unskilled or semi-skilled staff, towards more self-managing knowledge workers, the recent fashions for deskilling and downsizing, and the consequent decrease of organizational effectiveness and efficiency look increasingly silly.

In some organizations which are thinking deeply about their structure, processes and their emotional contracts with staff, these fashions are being turned on their head. Selecting and training staff and then leaving them to sink or swim in the changing dynamics of the organization is not an effective way to cope with rapid environmental change. Knowledge workers are an investment and should be treated, financially and emotionally, as such. The Organizational Capabilities of personal rewards, financial rewards, clarity of personal responsibility, personal, and group, performance indicators are all important here.

There is no doubt that, viewed only as a cost, people are expensive, but they are not just costs. They are also assets which can create new learning, intellectual property and skills, to increase the asset base and shareholders' returns. Inanimate assets are shown on the balance sheet and properly maintained, nurtured and depreciated, but we are only just learning how to do this with our investments in people. Most budgets simply do not have the headings to do this.

This will have to happen to prevent knowledge workers walking out to join better employers. The values of trust and loyalty need serious nurturing, which many of us still have neither the patience nor the skills to do.

Ironically, even obsolete skills can have a value to a modern organization. A good example is the Millennium Bug, or Y2K, problem. No one knows the exact number of computers that had to be reprogrammed, but there were hundreds of millions around the world, from massive financial-services-linked mainframes to embedded chips in household products. Most of the old computers were programmed in COBOL, a language assumed to be obsolete, and computer companies paid serious money to bring COBOL programmers out of retirement to do this work in a great hurry. Many fifty to seventy year olds were delighted with the boost in their retirement income, and many companies regretted that they did not ask more intelligently naive, discriminating, questions on the purchase of their computing systems.

So if we are to take seriously and make true the great organizational lie that 'our people are our greatest asset' we need to value them – financially and emotionally. As we enter the twenty-first century there are a few systems of selection, induction, inclusion, competence-building and personal development for employability where these ideas are taken seriously. Whether we ever see a reporting system to directors which contains the following trend lines and ratios, profit and loss items and balance sheet items is up to you.

Trendlines of our people usage for directors' critical review:

Staff age profiles
Staff diversity
Time in company
Time in department
Time in present job
Competence level in job
Qualifications
Satisfactorily completed appraisals
Levels of customer satisfaction
Levels of co-operating work-group satisfaction
Personal development actions
Absenteeism rate
Sickness rate
Turnover rate

These can be compiled easily for all staff, managers and directors.
On the profit and loss account there could be:

Wages/revenue ratio
Wages/profit ratio
Productivity/£s per employee
Selection costs
Induction, Inclusion, Competence-building costs
Absenteeism costs
Sickness costs
Turnover rate costs

and the adaptation of these to fit the evolving EFMD ratios suggested in chapter 1.

On the balance sheet we could see:
Assets:

People
Key players
Investment in learning
Investment in qualifications
Investment in personal development
Compliance levels in health and safety at work

Intellectual property rights:

Patents
Copyrights
Registered designs
Trademarks
Servicemarks
Trade secrets
Goodwill
Brands

Is this how we will measure and resolve the dilemma of achieving hard tasks through soft systems? Will we be able to ensure our Organizing Capabilities so that people and emotions matter? Will we be able to break the blame culture,[40] and develop our organizations as continuous learning systems? I think so. Then instead of relying on Henry Ford's complaint that 'When I hire a pair of hands I always get a person as well,' we can rejoice in the fact that 'When I hire a pair of hands I also get a free brain.' This is truly adding value to Organizational Capabilities and specific democratization of an organization.

Acknowledgements

My thanks go out to all those friends and clients who over the years just knew that organizations had to be better places to work in than they often are, and set out to do something about it.

At the risk of upsetting many for not mentioning them, I will list those who have had a major influence on my thinking. In the 1970s and 1980s Charles Handy, John Morris, Reg Revans, Tom Lupton, Alistair Mant, Denys Pym, Derek Pugh, Sue Birley, David Norburn, Tony Hodgson and John Stopford, all from the academic world, had a profound effect on me. The Developing Senior Managers Programme for General Electric Company had a deep and continuing influence on my approach, and I am especially indebted to Mike Bett, David Pearce, Geoff Gaines, John Shrigley, Hugh Allen, Glynn Trollope, Dick Clayton and Lord Weinstock for the access they gave me. The external action learning advisors to GEC were a particularly demanding and stimulating group who gave constructive, and often robust, criticism: so thanks to Jean Lawrence, David Casey, Tony Eccles, David Sutton, Alan Lawlor and Ian Cunningham; and to that unique trades union officer, John Lloyd, who gave us all an intellectual run for our money.

The diversity of ideas in this book owes much to continuing discussions with my consultancy partner Peter Barrett, in Hong Kong; and with such colleagues as Hai Chi Yuet in Hong Kong, Denise Fleming in Sydney, Ismael Mohamed in Brunei, Max Boisot in Barcelona, Chen De Rong in Shanghai and Geoffrey Bowes in Wellington. In the UK my consulting colleagues continue to debate with me and I am grateful to Janice Caplan,

Tontschy Gerig, Barry Paterson, Colin Hastings, Jean Roberts, Sue Thame, Jerry Rhodes and Frank Tyrrell for their interest.

Although I have worked with a number of financial services companies I am keen to thank the people at Lloyds TSB, who over a period of some eleven years allowed me deep access to the evolving corporation. I would like to thank particularly Sir Nicholas Goodison, Peter Ellwood, Theresa Barnett, Paul Turner, Gary Mann, Geoff Courts, Nick Wells and Alan Houston for their continuous support.

Amongst the many other colleagues who have helped my development I would like to thank Suzie Morel, Coralie Palmer, Chris Davies, David Moed, Bob Marks and the Institute of Directors team under John Harper, all of whom shared their experience and were willing to criticize ideas constructively and have helped make this a better book than the one I had intended originally.

Particular thanks go to Luciuda McNeile and Mike Fishwick for commissioning this book, and to Kate Morris who guided me superbly to its finish.

Notes

1. *Financial Times*, 2 January 1999
2. *Angle of Repose*, Wallace Stegner, Penguin Books, New York, 1971
3. *Concise Oxford Dictionary*
4. *Beyond World Class*, Clive Morton, Macmillan Business, London, 1998
5. London School of Economics, and Sheffield University, 1991–2001 study, London 1999
6. *EFMD Review* 9813, Brussels
7. *Brand Warriors*, Fiona Gilmore, HarperCollins*Business*, London 1997
8. *Corporate Amnesia*, Arnold Kransdorff, Butterworth Heinemann, Oxford, 1998
9. *Knowledge Assets*, Max Boisot, Oxford University Press, Oxford, 1998
10. *Obedience to Authority*, Stanley Milgram, Pinter & Martin 1964
11. *Dilbert*, Scott Adams, Harper*Business*, New York, 1997
12. *The New Office*, Francis Duffy, Conran Octopus, London 1997
13. *Financial Times*, 10 July 1996
14. *The Theory of Social and Economic Organization*, Max Weber, Berlin, 1924
15. *Moments of Truth*, Jan Carlzon, Ballinger, Cambridge, Mass., 1987
16. *The Fish Rots from the Head: The Crisis in Our Boardrooms*, Bob Garratt, HarperCollins*Business*, London, 1996

17. *Culture and Organizations: The Software of the Mind*, Geert Hofstede, HarperCollins*Business*, 1994

18. *Co-opetition*, A. Brandenberger & B. Nalebuff, HarperCollins, London, 1997

19. *The Learning Organization*, Bob Garratt, HarperCollins*Business*, London, 1987 – this book is being completely revised and will be republished in 2000 by Harper*Collins*

20. *The Strategy Safari*, Henry Mintzberg, Joe Lampel, Bruce Anisbrand, Jossey-Babs Inc, 1998

21. *Fashionable Nonsense: Postmodern Intellectuals' Abuse of Science*, Alan Sokal, Jean Bricmont, Picades Press, 1996

22. *The Emperor's Nightingale: Restoring the Integrity of the Corporation*, Robert A. G. Monks, Capstone, Oxford, 1998

23. *The Rise and Fall of Strategic Planning*, Henry Mintzberg, Free Press, New York, 1994

24. *The Games People Play*, Eric Berne, Andre Deutsch, London, 1996

25. *Work and the Nature of Man*, Frederick Herzberg, World Publishing, New York, 1996

26. *Emotional Intelligence*, Daniel Goleman, Bloomsbury, London, 1996

27. *The Economist*, 8 July 1998

28. *Managerial Attitudes and Performance*, L. W. Porter and E. E. Lawler, Richard D. Irwin, Illinois, 1968

29. *The Importance of Cultures*, Clifford Geertz, Basic Books, New York, 1973

30. *Competing for the Future*, G. Hamel and C. K. Prahalad, *Harvard Business Review*, Boston, 1994

31. *The ABC of Action Learning*, R. W. Revans, Chartwell Bratt, Lund, 1982

32. *The Fifth Discipline*, Peter Senge, Doubleday, New York, 1991

33. *The Service Profit Chain*, James L. Heskett, W Earl Sasser, & Leonard A Schlesinger, Free Press, 1997

34. European Foundation for Quality Management – Business

Excellence Model – details can be had from the British Quality Foundation, 32 Great Peter Street, London SW1, UK, tel. 0207 654 5000

35. *The Balanced Scorecard*, R. S. Kaplan & P. Norton, Harvard Business School Press, Boston, Mass., 1996

36. *The Individualized Corporation*, Sumantra Ghoshal & Christopher Bartlett, Heinemann, London, 1997

37. *The Ministry*, Peter Hartcher, HarperCollins*Business*, London, 1998

38. *Bad Land*, Jonathan Raban, Picador, London, 1997

39. *Tomorrow's Company Inquiry*, Royal Society of Arts, London, 1997

40. *Avoiding the Blame Culture*, Michael Pearn, Chris Mulrooney & Tim Payne, Gower, Aldershot, 1998

Index